UNITED STATES

OF

DYSFUNCTION

America's Political Crisis and
What Ordinary Citizens Can Do About It

CARL JARVIS

The United States of Dysfunction

America's Political Crisis and
What Ordinary Citizens Can Do About It

Carl J. Jarvis

1st edition

ISBN-10: 1-62264-008-X
ISBN-13: 978-1-62264-008-9

Published by:
BKSC Media Group
P.O. Box 667203
Houston, TX 77266

Printed in the United States of America

54278934520708145289

To Jill—
who made it possible

"My people are destroyed for lack of knowledge."

Hosea 4:6

"God hath made man upright;
but they have sought out many inventions."

Ecclesiastes 7:29

"Whatsoever ye do, do it heartily,
as to the Lord, and not unto men."

Colossians 3:23

TABLE OF CONTENTS

Introduction

Is America Governable?...................5

Part I

Origins and Symptoms:
A Recurring Pattern of Tyranny.................11

Uncontrolled Search and Seizure.....................13
Taxation Without Representation.................24
Disarmament of Free Citizens.....................33

Part II

Principles and Departures:
The Breakdown of Republican Institutions.....45

The Secret Thread of American Political History........47
Rotation in Office and Entrenched Incumbency..........70
Distribution and Concentration of Power...................89
Self-Government and the Permanent Campaign.......106

Part III

Ground Zero:
The Destruction of Republican Institutions
1910-1925.........................115

The Beginning of a Congressional Revolution...........118

The Rebirth of the Rotten Boroughs 131
The Development of a Matrix of Dictatorship.............145
The Growth of Legislative Blackmail 159
The Transformation of the Money Power....................174
The Rise of Government by Judiciary...........................194
The Triumph of Ideological Polarization 211

Part IV

Vision:
Government of, by, and for the People

Restored 233
The Citizen's Role in Self-Government 235

Conclusion

Are We Rome? 249

Notes 255

About the Author... 269

PREFACE

When I was growing up, I thought someday I would write the great American novel. For many years, I arranged my life to accommodate this dream.

But nothing ever came of it.

As I modeled my writing, I read many Tom Clancy novels and my focus started to shift.

Slowly, life began to imitate art: I joined the Navy, trained with Marines and SEALs, and finally—due to a number of factors—was recruited and joined the Naval Nuclear Propulsion Program.

The whole time, I still had the idea of writing the great American novel in the back of my mind.

Until I realized there was a bigger story to be told.

My first glimpse of the bigger story occurred when I took the oath of office to "protect and defend the Constitution" when I joined the Navy.

I began to sense that the story of the Constitution was the story that made the great American novel possible, because creative expression needs freedom to flourish.

That's how I first became interested in American constitutional history.

Around the time when I began to seriously consider writing a book like this, I attended an economics conference in Houston in May of 2006—just as the Housing Bubble of 2003-2007 was reaching its climax.

I remember sitting there, being overcome by nausea at the realization that I needed to find a new job, due to forces far beyond my control.

I remember driving home feeling overwhelmed by the sheer immensity of the crisis we faced as a country, which few understood at the time.

Since then, things have changed.

With the support of my wife, I left my job to research and write this book.

My job didn't survive the financial crisis anyway.

Meanwhile, my country—which I refuse to leave—has started to wake up to the dangers we face.

People are starting to see that we can't take our country for granted and end up happily ever after.

More and more, people are asking what can be done to save our country.

I believe this book contains a practical way of thinking—and a proposal—which address that very question.

iv   CARL JARVIS

INTRODUCTION

Is America Governable?

How did America become such a mess?

We're the most entrepreneurial society on earth, yet our entitlement programs are bankrupt.

We're among the most innovative nations in the world, yet our education system is in shambles.

We're a nation of immigrants, yet our immigration policy is broken.

We're among the wealthiest countries in the world, yet our economy is rife with fraud.

We're the mightiest superpower on the planet, yet that power is increasingly directed against our own citizens.

All may appear well for now, but we're rapidly careening toward a crisis of confidence that could rock the foundations of our political system.

With so many problems growing worse by the day, it's fair to ask what our political leaders have been up to.

Tune into the Sunday morning talk shows, and you'll hear endless posturing around the issues of the day.

Our leaders tell us "deficits don't matter" and "domestic spying is no big deal."

Our leaders tell us everything's under control.

But they don't seem to have a clue; and they won't publicly admit the reality of most problems we face.

Even to the extent that they acknowledge the real problems, they aren't doing anything about them.

These self-styled "defenders of the people" could not care less about your plight.

Their overriding purpose is to win reelection and to hold onto power at all costs.

Maybe that's how our country became such a mess.

* * *

As our country lurches from crisis to crisis, our leaders feed us talking points intended to sow division and discord among the people.

Washington has become a looking-glass world in which hot button, poll-driven issues are all that matter. The atmosphere is described as "polarized" and "toxic."

Political scientists William Galston and Peitro Nivola remark that "The U.S. Congress is more polarized ideologically [today] than it was just a generation ago."[1]

Columnist Ronald Brownstein observes that "the two parties now spend most days at each other's throats… contemporary Washington politics often seems the extension of war by other means."[2]

Thomas Mann and Norman Ornstein have documented "the decline of genuine deliberation in the lawmaking process…the manifestations of extreme partisanship; the culture of corruption…and the weakening of the checks-and-balances system."[3]

Fareed Zakaria has observed of modern Washington that, "The old party was rooted in neighborhoods, local government, and broad-based organizations…The new party is dominated by Washington professionals— activists, ideologues, fund raisers, pollsters."[4]

James Carville and Stan Greenberg concede that "Government has really screwed things up for the average American. Work has been devalued. Education costs are out of sight. Effort and ambition have never been so scantily rewarded." They go on to say, "Political parties must admit their failures and the electorate must reclaim its voice."[5]

The problem is that our entire political system has become, in the words of law professor Larry Lessig, "an engine of influence"[6] that enriches the politically connected at the expense of everyone else.

Lessig observes that "members of Congress spend between 30 and 70 percent of their time raising money... [and they have] a constant awareness about how what they do might affect their ability to raise money."[7]

People sense the political system is working against their interests. And they're increasingly disgusted.

In one recent report, Wang Jisi gives us a glimpse of one possible future in his portrayal of how Chinese leaders perceive the United States today:

America's financial disorder, alarming deficit and unemployment rate, slow economic recovery, and domestic political polarization are viewed as but a few indications that the United States is headed for decline...It is now a question of how many years, rather than how many decades, before China replaces the United States as the largest economy in the world.[8]

All of these observations add up to a disturbing picture. They portray an increasingly accepted consensus that things just aren't working here in the United States.

If you look deeper, there's even a consensus as to *why* things aren't working.

The reason *why* things aren't working is what this book is about.

* * *

Today America is at a fork in the road.

People are disgusted with the empty rhetoric of politicians whose talking points are little more than veiled apologies for an unsustainable status quo.

Meanwhile, our inability to resolve the challenges we face is causing people to lose faith in the very institutions we need in order to remain a free society.[9]

Congress's approval rating, for example, stands at an all-time low since tracking began in the early 1970s.[10]

While media pundits rake in millions fanning the flames of discontent, they have no more desire to deal with reality than the politicians.

At the extremes, there's a growing number who criticize the act of voting, who denounce the political parties without reservation, and who condemn the legislative institutions that lie at the heart of our republican form of government

There are others who see no good in the Constitution, and who say it needs to be radically amended—or even abolished—if we're to make our system work again.

This entire train of thought is contrary to our system of self-government, and pushes us toward tyranny.

The mood in America has reached a point that has seen charismatic leaders and men on horseback seize control in many less fortunate countries.

* * *

To diagnose the true nature of the crisis we face is not an easy or straightforward proposition.

The problems we see today have been growing and spreading for a very long time. To get to the root of these problems, we must first understand their nature. And to understand their nature, we must go back to the very beginning.

We must examine the political condition of our country from its early years through the present time.

Part I of this book looks at parallels between our present crisis and the policies that brought the American colonies to the brink of revolution in 1776.

Part II steps through a theory that I believe explains the origins of our present crisis. Without spoiling the story, the crisis is institutional and not ideological in nature, and it began around a hundred years ago.

Part III looks at the long-forgotten changes made to our institutions between 1910 and 1925, and links those changes to the many problems we face today.

Part IV looks at what we can do about our present crisis, beginning with the single, most effective action anyone can take—immediately—to begin restoring self-government in the United States.

The Conclusion looks at the consequences of our present crisis, if we were to do nothing about it.

* * *

To understand the crisis we face—a crisis that began with mere dysfunction, and which may end in tyranny— we must begin with a simple observation.

Historically, checks and balances were found not only in our Constitution, but in the political process as well.

Around a hundred years ago, political incumbents began to strip the checks and balances out of our system.

Today, we're living through the consequences, as we watch the economic power and moral leadership of the United States decline right before our eyes.

It's no coincidence that our declining economic power has coincided with a loss of liberty at home.

It's also no coincidence that we keep electing the same people over and over, and getting the same results.

It's time we figure out why.

It's time we restore the political institutions that made our country great.

And it's time we restore our constitutional checks and balances, before it's too late.

It's a big promise, yet I believe this book shows the way.

PART I

Origins and Symptoms: A Recurring Pattern of Tyranny

Why does it matter whether we're governed under rule of law? What difference does rule of law make, anyway?

In the simplest terms, rule of law shields the people from the arbitrary whims of rulers who would otherwise trample the liberties of ordinary citizens.

Because of this, the most important provisions of rule of law, in our country, are found in the Bill of Rights.

Thus, if greatness and goodness of our country stems from the liberties of the people, then the erosion of rule of law brings about the decline of everything that makes our country worth preserving.

Liberty and rule of law—the twin fountainheads of the greatness of America—have made our country different, unique, and exceptional throughout its history.

The liberty of America was a beacon to all mankind, since the very origins of our country, because it stood out from mankind's default condition, which is tyranny.

Rule of law secured our liberty and raised us above the inherent frailties of human nature.

Today, erosion of rule of law signifies a reversion to the mean, which threatens to condemn us to tyranny.

Tyranny is a strong word, and to merely utter the word does not clothe it in its full meaning.

Even to explain tyranny as John Locke did, as "the exercise of power beyond right, which no body can have a right to,"[1] doesn't quite get to the heart of the matter.

To truly understand tyranny is to appreciate it in a visceral sense, which is the way the framers of our Constitution and Bill of Rights understood it.

Acquiring a visceral sense of tyranny is actually not that hard. It requires only a basic recitation of the events that led to the American Revolution.

We're beginning at the American Revolution, and not at the later origin of our present crisis, because we need to define what's at stake.

We need to establish why any of what follows matters in the first place.

To explain the decline of our Constitution, there's no better place to begin than with the birth of America—and that series of events which still inform our country's reason for existence today.

1

Uncontrolled Search and Seizure

There is no surer sanction for limitless government power than uncontrolled search and seizure.

Uncontrolled search and seizure is the indispensable handmaiden of tyranny; a lynchpin of arbitrary rule so essential that no tyrant can afford to be without it.

No oppressive law can be enforced unless government first asserts an arbitrary power of search and seizure.

This is the condition the Fourth Amendment of the Constitution was intended to redress and prevent.

Yet, career politicians, judges, and bureaucrats tell us we must terminate this most essential right so we can remain secure.

Today, our *right* against unreasonable searches and seizures is among the most disregarded rights protected by our Constitution.

The question is whether we can bargain away this right to buy a little security, without sacrificing all of the other rights that make our country worth defending.

* * *

To understand the Fourth Amendment is to know why we have it in the first place, since its meaning and its existence derive from the same series of events. The experience of the Founders under the arbitrary rule of King George III placed the issue of uncontrolled search and seizure at the forefront of their concerns. Through experience, the Founders developed the view that the right of the people against unreasonable searches and seizures is among the chief safeguards of liberty.

We could go even further and propose that the Fourth Amendment is among the chief reasons why we have a United States Constitution in the first place.

The reason is simple: if you look at the origins of the revolutionary conflict that made America an independent nation, you find at the very root of the conflict the issue of uncontrolled search and seizure.

* * *

The "long train of abuses" that catalyzed American Independence began shortly after King George III ascended the throne.

In one of his first official acts, King George III renewed the authority of British officials to issue and use so-called "writs of assistance."

The writs of assistance were general search warrants issued by the colonial courts to enforce customs duties enacted by Parliament. They allowed customs officials to enter and search any property suspected of containing contraband. Rather than specifying the person or property to be searched, or the items to be seized, the warrants left these important details to the discretion of the officer to whom the writ had been issued.

Charles Paxton, a customs official in the Port of Boston, was among the officials who abused the writ. Paxton's abuse of the writs of assistance caused the merchants and property owners of Boston to unite in opposition against his arbitrary authority. The merchants' opposition resulted in the famous and celebrated *Writs of Assistance Case*, tried in Boston in February of 1761.

James Otis Jr. represented the merchants in the case. In so doing, Otis became among the first to put his life and fortune on the line by publicly adopting the cause of liberty against kingly oppression.

During five hours of impassioned argument, Otis condemned the writs of assistance as:

> Instruments of slavery on one hand and villainy on the other...the worst instrument of arbitrary power, the most destructive of English liberty and the fundamental principles of law, that ever was found in an English law-book.[1]

He denounced the power granted by the writs as one that "placed the liberty of every man in the hands of every petty officer."[2]

Although Otis lost the case, his argument created a sensation in Massachusetts's political circles and throughout the other colonies as well.

Among those in attendance that day was a young man who observed and took abundant notes of Otis's argument. The young man was John Adams.

Fifteen years later, on July 3, 1776—on the very eve of American Independence—John Adams wrote to his wife Abigail expressing his belief that, "[Otis's] Argument concerning Writs of Assistance...[was] the

Commencement of the Controversy, between Great Britain and America."[3]

The reasoning behind this belief was simple: the writs of assistance had given King George III the power to enforce any decree he or his ministers might conceive.

From the Stamp Act and Townshend duties, to the furtive and then overt disarmament of the colonists, arbitrary search and seizure was the King's primary means of enforcing his oppressive policies.

Shortly after American Independence, Adams would write Article XIV of the new Massachusetts state constitution, which read in part, "Every subject has a right to be secure from all unreasonable searches, and seizures of his person, his houses, his papers, and all his possessions."[4]

Similar provisions were written into other early state constitutions. North Carolina's constitution, for example, called the use of general warrants (like the writs of assistance) "dangerous to liberty." Virginia's constitution condemned the use of general warrants as "grievous and oppressive."[5]

All of these provisions would later inform the purpose, language, and intent of the Fourth Amendment.

* * *

Even a cursory look of the Fourth Amendment lays bare the absurd fearmongering of those who claim it jeopardizes our national security.

In truth, the Fourth Amendment *does not* deny government the power it needs to provide security.

What the Fourth Amendment *does* deny is an *uncontrolled* power of search and seizure. It does so through two important conditions it imposes on the search and seizure power.

First, the Fourth Amendment stipulates that "no Warrants shall issue, but upon probable cause, supported by Oath or affirmation." Second, it states that "no Warrants shall issue...[that do not] particularly [describe] the place to be searched, and the persons or things to be seized."

Thus the thrust of the Fourth Amendment is to prohibit the kind of general warrants that oppressed the very people who wrote our Constitution.

In an earlier day, these constitutional limitations on the search and seizure power were considered common sense precautions against the abuse of power.

Today, these limitations are trampled underfoot by politicians, judges, and bureaucrats alike.

They override these safeguards in the name of security and seem unfazed by the potential for abuse of power.

* * *

While we can find any number of practices that violate the Fourth Amendment today, they all share a common characteristic. They all involve the exercise of arbitrary discretion by government agents in the conduct of search and seizure operations.

These days, we tolerate domestic spying and other invasions of privacy via "sneak and peek" searches, National Security Letters, dragnet electronic surveillance, and even the permanent archiving of the personal data of every law-abiding American who uses the internet.

Under any plain interpretation, every one of these practices is a blatant violation of the Fourth Amendment.

Yet all of these practices are allowed to continue under the authority of acts of Congress, many of which have been sustained by court rulings.

Today, these practices reach far into the private lives of American citizens who show no evidence or suspicion of wrongdoing.

We should prayerfully consider the consequences to which these practices have led, both here—during the revolutionary period—and in other countries since then.

The mere knowledge that these practices exist has a chilling effect on the exercise of all rights and freedoms, not least of which is the right of political dissent.

* * *

The USA PATRIOT Act is a case study in the systematic stripping away of the Fourth Amendment's safeguards in recent years.

There are three major provisions of the Patriot Act that undermine the Fourth Amendment: the so-called "library records" provision, the "sneak and peak" search provision, and the National Security Letter provision.

Under the "library records" provision, the Patriot Act authorizes federal law enforcement to obtain a variety of business records upon application to a judge, simply on the assertion that the investigation involves "international terrorism or clandestine intelligence activities."

It's called the "library records" provision because of the wide range of personal material that it permits law enforcement to obtain, without meaningful judicial oversight.

Law enforcement "information requests" under the "library records" provision are subject to a gag order, which means in practice that such requests are not disclosed to the person whose information is obtained.

We know this provision of the Patriot Act has been used to obtain the information of persons who are not the actual subjects of investigation.

Next, under the "sneak and peak" search provision of the Patriot Act, federal law enforcement is authorized to conduct secret searches without ever notifying the property owner or suspected individual.

What the law actually says is that notice of the warrant "may be delayed," but in practice the notice of the warrant may be delayed indefinitely.

Although there's judicial oversight in the issuance of "sneak and peak" warrants, it's debatable whether this is enough to prevent the abuse of power.

Lastly, under the "National Security Letter" provision of the Patriot Act, federal law enforcement agents are authorized to handwrite their own search warrants.

This means that National Security Letters are written entirely at the discretion of law enforcement, without any judicial oversight or due process whatsoever.

Although National Security Letters existed prior to the Patriot Act, the Patriot Act greatly expanded their authorized use to allow law enforcement to obtain financial and telephone records of individuals without a warrant issued by a judge.

We know from congressional reports that federal law enforcement issues tens of thousands of National Security Letters every year, which includes thousands to obtain the records of American citizens.

Furthermore, we know National Security Letters are not necessarily used to obtain *only* the records of the subjects of investigation, but are also used to obtain the records of people with whom a subject of investigation may have been in contact in the past.

The use of National Security Letters to obtain information and evidence, without judicial oversight, very much lends itself to abuse of power.

Each of these practices authorized by the Patriot Act is a plain and blatant violation of the Fourth Amendment.

* * *

As if the Patriot Act's disregard for the Fourth Amendment were not enough, the last twelve years have witnessed the rise of a vast dragnet surveillance apparatus under the watchful gaze of the National Security Agency (NSA).

In late 2005, *New York Times* journalists James Risen and Eric Lichtblau broke the story of NSA's Operation Stellar Wind, a warrantless surveillance program so boundless that it could not possibly exclude the personal communications of law-abiding American citizens.[6]

Risen and Lichtblau reported that immediately after 9/11, the Bush administration established the program as a way to bypass the negligible warrant requirements of the Foreign Intelligence Surveillance Act of 1978 (FISA).

With the outcry that ensued after the program was revealed, Congress passed the FISA Amendments Act of 2008. Through the new law, Congress legalized the existing program while granting retroactive immunity to companies and persons that had participated.

Essentially, the law allowed unchecked surveillance to continue without meaningful oversight, under a program whose scale is inconceivable to most Americans.

Shortly after NSA programs were legalized and returned to supervision under the FISA Court, NSA began its PRISM domestic spying program.

In June of 2013, Glenn Greenwald of *The Guardian* began publishing a series of revelations about the PRISM program, and several related programs, which were brought to light by NSA contractor-turned-whistleblower Edward Snowden.[7]

The scope of PRISM, and its deep integration into private internet infrastructure, is truly staggering.

The program collects all emails, chats, videos, photos, stored data, file transfers, login activity, social network connections, and other information, directly from internet service providers such as Microsoft, Google, Yahoo!, Facebook, Skype, AOL, Apple, and others.

Upon collection, the program permanently archives all records, presumably in the multibillion-dollar data center NSA is building in the Utah desert.

The conclusion we can draw from these disclosures is that everything you do on the Internet—practically every keystroke—is being warehoused and made searchable whenever the government wants, and for whatever purpose a government agent may conceive.

NSA and other federal agencies are currently collecting so much information on every man, woman, and child in America that it's impossible for the information to be analyzed and used to fight terrorism in real time.

What's even more troubling—especially given recent revelations about the Internal Revenue Service's targeting of citizens' groups, and the Justice Department's seizure of Associated Press journalists' records—is the spectacular abuse of power made possible by such a vast archive of private records.

Even supposing the best intentions, the mere archiving of the information—making it available *for any reason, and at any time in the future*—is questionable.

Given the frailty of human nature—especially when mere mortals are entrusted with absolute power—the mass archiving of records is downright scary.

It doesn't take much imagination to see how the data might be abused.

The sheer volume of information being collected and archived would have been the dream of many totalitarian rulers throughout history.

* * *

The problem of uncontrolled search and seizure has become so pervasive that it's no longer a problem that can be dealt with by the courts.

Even if the Supreme Court mustered the courage to strike down one of these secret surveillance programs, it's likely the operations would continue in the shadows.

Thus the problem is not legal in nature, but political.

We're told by our representatives in Congress—most of whom don't bother to read the bills they vote on—that we need these programs for our safety and security.

Whether these programs enhance our security against foreign enemies has never been demonstrated.

Meanwhile, given the way the data is being collected and archived, it's clear the programs can be used against American citizens on a whim and without restraint.

We can talk all day long about how these practices are indistinguishable from the writs of assistance so despised by our forefathers.

But the real problem we are dealing with is more elemental than that: it is a question of power and power cannot be tamed by reason.

Not coincidentally, the same politicians who vote to expand these programs without limit are the career politicians who seek to perpetuate *their own power* without limit.

With this in mind, the true concern behind these programs becomes clear. They're simply the political class's way of saying: We hold the power, and we defy you to do something about it.

2

Taxation Without Representation

The circulation of ordinary citizens between public office and private life is the vital principle of our republican form of government.

With the expectation of a return to private life, politicians don't develop the delusions of grandeur that so many of them have today.

But in thinking of this principle, those who formed our first state constitutions committed an error.

They merely repeated the old Whig maxim: "where ANNUAL ELECTIONS end, TYRANNY begins."[1]

But the true principle can be more accurately put: "where ROTATION IN OFFICE ends, TYRANNY begins."

Today, we know better than to think that elections will prevent tyranny from taking root.

Tyranny is checked in an elective system only so long as elected officials *as a class* regularly return to private life, to live under the laws and policies they enact.

Today it's hard to imagine, but there was a time when elected officials' frequent return to private life was the unwritten law of the land.

CARL JARVIS

Today we have elections, but it's not uncommon for an elected official to serve for twenty or thirty years—or more—*sometimes even in the same office.*

Today we have elections, but scarcely a meaningful power to remove incumbents from office.

* * *

Two distinct theories of representation inform how we think about elections.

The first theory—primitive in origin—holds that people are represented by inhabiting a place, regardless of their power to select or remove their representatives.

The second theory—which developed alongside our republican form of government—holds that people are represented only when they may withhold consent from the making of laws with which they must comply.

Each of these theories has bearing on our political condition today.

Today we ask: Do we have elections to lend legitimacy to whatever laws our representatives may deign to enact? Or do we have elections so the people can express disapproval—and withhold consent—from laws and taxes they find obnoxious?

Given the events surrounding the creation of our Constitution, it's clear that it was formed with the second theory in mind.

Thus our elective system was established to preserve the consent of the governed, by empowering the people to hold their representatives accountable.

* * *

In the split between Britain and America that resulted in American Independence, the conflict over the Stamp Act was among the important seminal events.

Through the writs of assistance, King George III claimed an arbitrary power to enforce whatever decrees or laws he or his ministers might conceive. It remained to be seen to what use that power would be put.

In 1765, four years after the *Writs of Assistance Case*, the King's ministers in Parliament passed the Stamp Act.

The Act was to "[defray] the expense of defending, protecting, and securing" the American colonies.

The tax was to impose a levy on nearly every legal and financial transaction in the colonies, from bills of lading to mortgages. It also taxed a bizarre litany of printed items such as diplomas, playing cards, and almanacs.

Despite the colonists' lack of direct representation in Parliament, the Stamp Act met resistance.

As one parliamentarian said of the Act's stated aim:

They protected by *your* Arms? they have nobly taken up Arms in your defense, have Exerted a Valour amidst their constant and Laborious industry for the defense of a Country, whose frontier, while drench'd in blood, its interior Parts have yielded all its little Savings to [you].[2]

Even those who wrote the Stamp Act tacitly acknowledged the oppressiveness of the new tax.

In the provision for its enforcement, the Stamp Act denied the American colonists the right of trial by jury, so concerned were the authors of the Act that juries would nullify the new tax.

This abridgement of the right of trial by jury was among the colonists' grievances against King George III listed in the Declaration of Independence.

The colonists began a vigorous resistance to the Stamp Act the moment it passed, even though it was not scheduled to take effect until seven months afterward.

On both sides of the Atlantic, pamphleteers squared off with opposing arguments.

Out of this polemical exchange, the theory of *virtual representation* was born.

As one pro-Stamp Act pamphleteer put it, "[the colonists] claim it is a true Privilege, which is common to all *British* Subjects, of being taxed only with their Consent."[3]

After alluding to the vast majority of the "People of Britain" who had no say whatsoever in the election of Parliament, the writer asserted that "All *British* Subjects are really in the same: none are actually, all are virtually represented in Parliament."[4]

Although the doctrine of virtual representation was claimed in all apparent sincerity, it remained to be seen whether the Americans would accept the doctrine.

To lend greater weight to their objections, the colonists resolved to convoke an assembly of *actual* representatives. The assembly became known as the Stamp Act Congress.

The Stamp Act Congress was convened in mid-October of 1765, just two weeks before the Stamp Act was scheduled to take effect.

The delegates found a ready consensus, and the resolutions of the Stamp Act Congress were diplomatic but forceful.

The colonists proclaimed their "Allegiance to the Crown" and "due Subordination to…the Parliament of *Great-Britain*."[5]

Following these pleasantries, however, the colonists held forth the doctrine that "no Taxes be imposed on them, but with their own Consent."[6]

This ancient doctrine had stood the test of centuries of English constitutional development; it had emerged as an essential bulwark of republican liberty.

Out of this ancient doctrine sprang the colonists' rallying cry: No taxation without representation.

Although the Stamp Act Congress could not repeal the law, its resolves steeled the colonists in their defiance of the new tax.

As the Stamp Act went into effect, it soon became a byword for the perils of taxing and legislating without the consent of the people.

At first, the Stamp Act caused a mild decline in business activity, as the colonists refused to transact under the terms of the law.

After a few months, however, the stamp tax was ignored. As one historian put it, "a gradual nullification of the statute took place"[7] since the colonists went on with their business as if the law didn't exist.

To the extent British authorities were able to enforce the tax on goods imported from Britain, the colonists refused to purchase those items.

The boycott caused a general decline in the business activity of Britain. Soon, British merchants were petitioning Parliament to repeal the Stamp Act.

These efforts resulted in the repeal of the Act after it had been in force for less than six months.

From beginning to end, the Stamp Act episode demonstrates the futility of a government imposing taxes without the consent of the people.

These early developments seem to suggest that the principle of "no taxation without representation" had prevailed over "virtual representation."

But events had not yet run their course. Although the crisis passed with the Stamp Act's repeal, the doctrine of virtual representation did not.

The same day Parliament repealed the Stamp Act, Parliament also enacted the Declaratory Act.

Through the Declaratory Act, Parliament claimed for itself an unspecified power to "bind the colonies and people of *America*...in all cases whatsoever."

Like King George III's assertion of power through writs of assistance, it remained only to be seen to what use this limitless power would be put.

But it didn't take long for the colonists to find out.

Within just a few years, they were again subjected to oppressive taxation.

This time, however, Parliament authorized the quartering of troops in homes and the King quietly ordered the confiscation of firearms to enforce the tax.

Thus the arrogance of power which arose in tandem with the doctrine of virtual representation led to the open rebellion that followed.

* * *

Although Congress has yet to pass a law to "bind... the people of *America*...in all cases whatsoever," Congress has shown a similar degree of arrogance in recent years.

Not least among such displays was the passage of the Patient Protection and Affordable Care Act (also known as "Obamacare").

Few laws in our nation's history have been more disdainful toward the natural law of supply and demand.

Few laws in our nation's history have usurped more power from ordinary people over matters concerning their own lives.

Although Obamacare is not yet fully implemented, it's already causing the kind of rate increases, service interruptions, and exodus from the medical profession predicted well in advance by the bill's detractors.

On top of all of this, no law ever in our nation's history has imposed a tax to penalize a person's refusal to purchase a good or service, as Obamacare does. Incidentally, the tax did not even originate in the House of Representatives, as required by the Constitution.

Thus no law in our nation's history has brought us closer to discovering first hand whether a government can give the people everything they want, without taking from them everything they have.

If the arrogance evident in Obamacare bears comparison to the Stamp Act episode of our early history, the parallels run deeper when you consider the common root of the arrogance in both cases.

While it's often claimed that Obamacare was created to help the poor, it remains to be seen whether it will help the poor, or whether it will merely enrich the pharmaceutical, health insurance, and other entrenched interests that supported its passage.

What *is* certain is that the law will generate an endless stream of subsidies and regulations, subject to the influence of members of Congress of both parties.

Over time (if not immediately), those subsidies and regulations will favor the same special interests that members of Congress must implore in order to fund their reelection campaigns.

In fact, it's fair to ask to what degree the final form of the Affordable Care Act was influenced by fundraising motives. It appears the law, in its final form, was influenced far more by fundraising motives than it was by concern for the interests of ordinary people.

The ugly truth about congressional elections today is that they're decided by money, not by people.

As long as incumbents do what is necessary to raise money, it's almost impossible for any challenger to dislodge them from office.

The upshot of this is that voters are left without a real choice, because they cannot withhold consent from obnoxious laws by electing new representatives.

In fact, given the way congressional elections work today, it's fair to ask whether the real purpose of Obamacare wasn't to provide endless fuel for the corrupt "engine of influence" that members of Congress use to raise money and perpetuate themselves in office.

Whatever may be the case, Obamacare is precisely the kind of arrogant law the people get when they have no real power to hold their representatives accountable.

* * *

In the spring of 2013, a flurry of reports claimed that Congress was moving to exempt its members and staff from the requirement to enroll in Obamacare.

While one news outlet dismissed the reports as "unbelievable,"[8] no credible denial that such talks had taken place was ever issued.

In any case, given the condition of congressional elections today, it would be *more* unbelievable if such talks had *not* taken place.

It's worth noting that at the time, the law was nowhere near being fully implemented.

Even the plausible notion that Congress would think of giving itself such an exemption summarizes, in a nutshell, everything that is wrong with our system today.

The idea that members of Congress would exempt themselves from a debacle of their own making—while leaving ordinary people to bear the burden of the law—speaks to a great fear that many people have today.

Increasingly, we live under a system that elevates elected officials above the people they purport to serve.

In the final analysis, the question isn't whether Congress would do such a thing as exempt itself.

The question is whether they could get away it.

The question is whether you, dear voter, would be able to do anything about it.

3

Disarmament of Free Citizens

The right to bear arms is born of the natural right of self-preservation—a fundamental human right no government can legitimately infringe.

The right to bear arms is also a vital principle of the republican theory which informed the creation of our Constitution.

Along with rotation in office and the balance of power, classical republican theory holds that there's no greater security for a free people than the right to bear arms.

This is why we have the Second Amendment.

Yet today we find ourselves in a *debate* about the meaning of the Second Amendment, the thrust of which is to deny its plain intent.

Today, politicians talk about the right to bear arms as if it were theirs to dispose of as they please.

We're told by the same politicians who see no limit to their *own* power that the right to bear arms no longer applies to the conditions of our society.

But the real question is whether we'd long remain a free society, if the people were once deceived into surrendering their right to bear arms.

There are several ways to arrive at a due appreciation of the Second Amendment and the right to bear arms.

We can look at the genealogy of the Second Amendment and trace its language to the events and grievances that prompted its adoption.

We can compare the language of the Second Amendment to other provisions of the Bill of Rights.

Or, we can simply examine the right to bear arms from the standpoint of classical republican theory.

Remarkably, these paths all lead to the same conclusion.

From this vantage point, it is clear the Second Amendment was not intended to protect the right of citizens to hunt or to shoot for sport.

Rather, the right to bear arms was intended to allow free citizens to defend themselves against violence and oppression, by force of arms if necessary.

* * *

Even as the Stamp Act was being repealed in early 1766, King George III was laying plans for a more concerted assault against the liberties of the American colonists.

A year later, Parliament renewed its efforts to tax the colonies with the Townshend Revenue Act, which imposed a tax on many imported items, such as glass, paper, paint, and tea.

With the renewal of "taxation without representation," the anger of the colonists was revived, especially in the trading Port of Boston.

To put down the rebellion that ensued, and to collect the tax, King George III sent troops to Boston.

With the British army on its way, patriots gathered at Faneuil Hall to determine a course of action.[1]

Among their resolves, they mentioned a disingenuous concern about the possibility of war with France; and they appealed to their countrymen to arm themselves. As justification for this call to action, the patriots cited a Massachusetts law which summoned households to equip themselves with a "well fix'd Firelock, Musket, Accountrements, and Ammunition."[2]

The patriots also cited the English Bill of Rights of 1689, which is part of the body of statutes that make up the English Constitution.

As law, the English Bill of Rights guaranteed and protected the colonists' rights as Englishmen no differently than if they'd been inhabitants of Britain.

As a record of historical grievances, the English Bill of Rights recalled events that gave the colonists reason to cleave to their firearms, with a wary eye toward tyranny.

The English Bill of Rights was a legacy of the Glorious Revolution of 1688, by which King James II had been removed from the English throne.

The list of grievances in the Bill of Rights was lengthy, and many of the grievances had to do with the infringement of religious freedom.

One of the grievances concerned the King's efforts to disarm the country's inhabitants.

Historically, the right to bear arms in England had been more a privilege than a right.

Even before the King's abuses, private ownership of firearms was confined to wealthy landowners who enjoyed the privilege of hunting on their own lands.

Even so, during the 1660s and 1670s, King Charles II moved to bar the common people of England from owning any firearms at all.

James II took disarmament a step further when he became King. He began building a Catholic standing army, while disarming the country's Protestants.

This policy, among others, gave rise to the revolution that ended in his removal from the throne.

The King's brazen disarmament policy is recalled by the English Bill of Rights, which read in part:

> that the raising or keeping of a standing army...in time of peace...is against law; [and] that the subjects which are Protestants, may have arms for their defence...as allowed by law...³

* * *

As the crisis in the colonies unfolded, it's remarkable how many well-known events revolved around British attempts to disarm the American colonists.

The game of cat and mouse began immediately after the British army arrived in Boston.

Tensions between the army and the colonists rose as the result of several confrontations, at least one of which involved civilian casualties.

The conflict came to a head when British officials refused to allow three shiploads of tea to be returned to England.

The colonists responded by dumping the tea into the harbor, an event known today as the Boston Tea Party.

Parliament reacted by passing the Intolerable Acts, which blockaded Boston harbor, authorized the quartering of troops in homes, and stripped the province of Massachusetts of self-rule.

From this point forward, Boston was effectively in a stage of siege under martial law.

As the hostilities escalated, the British intensified their efforts to deny arms to the colonists, while the colonists redoubled their smuggling of arms into the countryside.

In September of 1774, British troops seized a magazine just outside Boston and confiscated the gunpowder stored inside. Tensions were so high that the incident raised an alarm that spread to the surrounding states.

As British policy shifted from restricting imports to outright confiscation, efforts to disarm the colonists brought the two sides ever closer to war.

Finally, the disarmament policy resulted in the "shot heard 'round the world," which marked the beginning of the War of Independence.

In the series of events recalled in the lore of Paul Revere's midnight ride, the objective of the British army was to seize arms and ammunition that were being stockpiled around Lexington and Concord.

Although the Americans outmatched the British in the Battle of Lexington and Concord, the British policy of disarmament was having its effect.

As Abigail Adams wrote shortly after the Battle of Bunker Hill, "Courage I know we have in abundance, conduct I hope we shall not want, but powder—where shall we get a sufficient supply?"[4]

* * *

Disarmament was British policy throughout the American colonies, and was by no means confined to the province of Massachusetts.

The experience of disarmament—and the distress and powerlessness that came with it—was seared into the minds of the framers of our Constitution.

Among the grievances listed in the Declaration of Independence was that King George III "kept among us, in Times of Peace, Standing Armies...[and he] affected to render the Military independent of and superior to the Civil Power."

The reference to standing armies and subordination of the military to civil authority not only called to mind the English Bill of Rights, but also anticipated the carefully crafted provisions of the first state constitutions.

In language that prefigured the Second Amendment, Pennsylvania's first state constitution guaranteed, "That the people have a right to bear arms for defence of themselves and the state..."[5]

The provision further declared that:

> standing armies in the time of peace are dangerous to liberty [and] ought not to be kept up; And the military should be kept under strict subordination to, and governed by, the civil power.[6]

Virginia's first state constitution contained similar language:

> standing armies, in time of peace, should be avoided as dangerous to liberty; and...in all cases the military should be under strict subordination to, and governed by, the civil power.[7]

This language hearkened back to the English Bill of Rights and to the Declaration of Independence.

Thus by the time the Bill of Rights was written in 1789, there was a long chain of precedents not only upholding the right to bear arms, but also attesting to its necessity.

Because the Second Amendment was written with such brevity, it's almost impossible to fully appreciate its significance without reference to the chain of precedents that inform its meaning.

The Second Amendment's preamble, "A well regulated Militia, being necessary to the security of a free State" is best understood alongside the warnings against standing armies long associated with the right to bear arms.

Classical republican theory held that the "security of a free State" could *not* be maintained if entrusted *exclusively* to a standing army; the army would gain the power to usurp civil authority without a citizen militia.

Thus the "Militia" was to stand as a bulwark against the threat of "standing armies."[8]

We could delve deeper into the intent of the "Militia" clause and suppose, as Virginia's first constitution did, "That a well regulated militia, composed of the body of the people, trained to arms, is the proper, natural and safe defence of a free state…"[9]

In others words, the "well-regulated Militia" may well have been intended to render a standing army unnecessary for the defense of the country.

* * *

Today, we're told that the very idea of a citizen militia is outmoded if not absurd, and that social conditions have changed the meaning of the Second Amendment.

Thankfully, to refute the error in this thinking, we don't have to resort to the Second Amendment's genealogy or to the republican theory of standing armies.

All that's needed is to read the plain language of the Second Amendment alongside other provisions of the Bill of Rights.

The word "Militia," for example, appears in the Second and Fifth Amendments. In the Fifth Amendment, the language is, "the Militia, when in actual service." The Second Amendment's use of the word "Militia" is unqualified; this implies that it refers to an armed citizenry in general, and not to a select militia or other government-sponsored group.[10]

The phrase "the right of the people" is found in the First, Second, and Fourth Amendments. Since it would be absurd to claim that the First and Fourth Amendments don't protect individual rights, it is similarly absurd to claim that the Second Amendment doesn't protect the individual right to keep and bear arms.[11]

Perhaps most interesting of all is the phrase "shall not infringe." It appears *only* in the Second Amendment. This phrase can be contrasted with "Congress shall make no law," which originally made the First Amendment applicable only to acts of Congress.[12]

The phrase "shall not infringe" is broad enough that it applies even to state and local governments that might deny the individual right to keep and bear arms.

These provisions all show a clear intent by the framers of the Second Amendment to secure the *individual's* right to bear arms; and this was the undisputed interpretation of the Second Amendment throughout the first century of its existence.

* * *

If the plain language of the Second Amendment is thought insufficient to establish its meaning, then let's return again to the classical republican theory that informed the creation of our Constitution.[13]

Plato and Aristotle, in particular, represent opposing sides in a debate over the right to bear arms that's taken place since the birth of political philosophy.

In fact, the views of Plato and Aristotle shed far more light on the controversy than anything the Constitution says—or *could* say—about the right to bear arms.

To begin with, Plato's entire theory of a republic was really a concealed defense of totalitarianism.

In *The Republic*, Plato suggests that "for subjects to do what was commanded by their rulers is just." He equates justice with "the interest of the stronger...[who] may command the weaker who are his subjects."[14]

Further along in *The Republic*, after making his ruling class of guardians the soldiery of the state, Plato says, "That the soldier who leaves his rank or throws away his arms...should be degraded into the rank of a husbandman or artisan."[15]

This passage suggests that Plato—not unlike our modern philosopher-kings—categorically opposed the right of the common people to keep and bear arms.

Meanwhile, Aristotle's inquiry into the "best form of government" led him to a form which he called "polity."

Aristotle's polity is the ideal form which the framers of our Constitution sought to make real two thousand years later. Of this "polity" form of government, Aristotle said:

> The whole set-up is intended to be neither democracy nor oligarchy but midway between the two—which is called 'polity,' *because it consists of those who bear arms.*[16]

Thus the opposing ideals of Plato and Aristotle suggest that the right to bear arms is needed to preserve the *spirit*—if not the *form*—of our republican institutions.

In fact, *modern republicanism* originated five hundred years ago when the common people of England and Europe began to throw off the yoke of absolute rule.

Machiavelli lived at a time when firearms began to alter the balance of power between princes and the common people. In *The Prince*, he observed that armed citizens are less inclined to submit to petty tyrants and that "where they are well armed they have good laws."[17]

In *Democracy in America*, Tocqueville remarked that "the invention of firearms equalized the vassal and the noble on the field of battle."[18]

Is it a coincidence, then, that the absolute power of despotic monarchs began to wane, as firearms became available to the common people?

As kings and princes lost their monopoly on force, they could no longer rule without the consent of the people, and modern constitutional republics were born.

* * *

The right of ordinary citizens to keep and bear arms is among the very few essential bulwarks needed to preserve our republican institutions.

The right of the people to bear arms is the right that guards all other rights, because it's the last security the people have against tyranny.

The ugly truth is that disarmament of peaceful and law-abiding citizens has been repeated again and again throughout history.

Disarmament is often the final step before a tyrant unleashes untold terror on the people.

Along these lines, we need hardly mention Hitler disarming the Jews, or Mao and Stalin confiscating firearms from the peasants.[19]

With history as a guide, we need to be *extremely wary* of policies that give government officials the arbitrary power to *deny* the people the right to bear arms. Some may scoff at the idea of ordinary people taking up arms in defense against the designs of a tyrant.

The Second Amendment is thus an uncomfortable reminder of the people's last resort, when all other sanctions against violence and oppression have failed.

PART II

Principles and Departures: The Breakdown of Republican Institutions

The Bill of Rights is a dead letter without checks and balances on political power.

This truth was well recognized by the framers, who did not include a Bill of Rights in the original Constitution.

Alexander Hamilton argued in *Federalist* no. 84 that the "structure of the government" would serve as the primary bulwark of individual liberties, and that "the constitution is itself...A BILL OF RIGHTS."[1]

James Madison similarly argued in *Federalist* nos. 25 and 48 that "parchment provisions" and "parchment barriers" would be sacrificed to "public necessity," unless made enforceable by means of checks and balances.[2]

But this is not to claim, as Hamilton and Madison did at first, that the Bill of Rights is unnecessary or useless.

What we can say is that the Bill of Rights is effective in securing liberty *only to the extent that its provisions are enforced as law.* But such enforcement depends on the existence of a distribution of political power that is not provided by the Bill of Rights itself.

In addition, the balance of power needed to preserve the Bill of Rights is more easily proposed on paper than achieved in reality.

As our present condition attests, the checks and balances contained in the Constitution are not enough to secure the balance of power.

In fact, the checks and balances in the Constitution have never been enough.

That's because the Constitution *never did contain the most important checks and balances*, many of which developed long after the Constitution was formed.

These "extra-constitutional" checks and balances—so often overlooked—have done the real work of preserving the balance of power throughout our history.

If our Constitution is neglected today—and our Bill of Rights ignored—we must look at the reality of how political power is distributed to fully understand *why*.

We must examine how the distribution of power changed so dramatically over a hundred year period when the Constitution changed hardly at all.

This requires that we go beyond conventional wisdom. It requires that we look at fundamental root causes— causes which will be found in the evolution of political institutions that lie outside the Constitution itself.

4

The Secret Thread of American Political History

The secret thread of American political history is the history of the nominating process we've used to select candidates for elected office in the United States.

Among the "extra-constitutional" checks and balances not contained in the Constitution, the nominating process is *by far* the most important.

And in the overthrow of our Constitution over the last one hundred years, *changes* to the nominating process have been the *greatest* single factor.

In fact, the history of the nominating process is the absolute, fundamental key to understanding how our political process has become so dysfunctional.

This is because—as we'll explore throughout this book—the effects of the nominating process can be seen throughout our entire political system.

Because the nominating process is the key to understanding what's happening to our country today, we'll begin here with an account of the history of the nominating process.

We'll look at the history of the nominating process mainly from the standpoint of the presidency, for two reasons.

First, the presidency—being the most powerful office in the country—shows the perilous effects of our current nominating process at an extreme.

Second, the excessive power of the presidency presents the single greatest opportunity to restore the checks and balances once furnished by our nominating process.

The purpose of this chapter is not to exhaust the annals of presidential history, but rather to establish the basic storyline that lies at the heart of this book.

* * *

The history of the nominating process in the United States can be roughly divided into three periods.

The first period began with the ratification of the Constitution and ended in the mid-1820s. During this first period, a mode of nomination known as the legislative caucus system prevailed.

Under the legislative caucus system, nominations to statewide office were decided by caucuses within the legislatures; members of Congress were similarly nominated by legislature; and presidential candidates were nominated by the "congressional caucus" system.

In presidential politics, the end of the first period was marked by the breakdown of the congressional caucus system in 1824.

The second period thus began in the late 1820s and continued until the first decade of the twentieth century. During this second period, a mode of nomination known as the party convention system prevailed.

Under the party convention system, candidates for nearly all elected offices in the country were nominated as the result of deliberations within party conventions.

In presidential politics, the second period came to an end when deliberations within the party conventions were undermined by the direct primary. The third period—which began in the early twentieth century—continues today. During this third period, the direct primary has been the prevailing mode of nomination.

Under the direct primary, candidates' names appear on the primary ballot. Many people believe this allows ordinary citizens to directly nominate candidates in the primary election, but we'll debunk this myth in due time.

It's not that party conventions ceased during this third period; we still hold conventions, at least in a nominal sense, but conventions have become irrelevant vestiges within the candidate selection process.

In presidential politics, we're still living with the direct primary system today. This fact has a number of implications that are worth exploring.

The periods of the nominating process are distinguished not only by the degree of "directness" in the mode of nomination, but also by the effects of each selection process on the distribution of power.

Thus the nominating process has affected the distribution of power between the *branches* of government; it has also affected the distribution of power between the federal and state *levels* of government.

The structure of the nominating process is important because it affects not only who our leaders are, but also how they're selected, including the types of appeals they make, the amount of money they need, and the advantage they enjoy as incumbents once elected.

The history of the nominating process is sometimes confused with the history of the Electoral College. This is because similar principles apply to the mode of election as well as to the mode of nomination.

Just as the history of the nominating process can be divided into three parts, the evolution of the Electoral College can be divided into three distinct periods as well.

The history of the Electoral College can be divided into pre- and post-Twelfth Amendment periods, with the dividing line at the election of 1800.

Before the Twelfth Amendment, the method of voting in the Electoral College worked against organized parties. The Twelfth Amendment changed that: it required "distinct ballots"[1] for the president and vice president in the Electoral College, which accommodated party-line voting in presidential elections.

The post-Twelfth Amendment period can be further divided into two periods, with the dividing line around the election of 1828. Prior to 1828, a few states continued to allow the state legislatures to appoint presidential electors. After 1828, every state except South Carolina used popular elections to choose presidential electors.

Because of their early coevolution, the nominating process and the Electoral College cannot be fully understood apart from one another.

* * *

The framers of the Constitution had no concept of a nominating process—for the presidency or for lesser offices—and no discernment of the need for one.

Yet interestingly, the framers' discussion of indirect elections touched on several issues that would later be resolved only through development of the nominating process.

At the heart of the framers' concerns was that the electorate would divide its votes between too many candidates, and presidential elections would become inconclusive and frequently disputed.

During one discussion, Charles Pinkney listed a number of problems with direct elections in general, including "disputed elections...which would be attended with intolerable expense and trouble."[2]

In another discussion of direct elections for the presidency, Roger Sherman observed that, "the people...will never give a majority of votes to any one man."[3]

The framers were especially concerned that disputed presidential elections, if frequent, would foster instability and perhaps even lead to the breakup of the Union.

To prevent inconclusive elections, they created the indirect mode of election we call the Electoral College.

Ironically, the Electoral College is despised today by proponents of direct popular election of the presidency, even though the system never worked as an indirect mode of election.

Because the Constitution requires presidential electors to "meet in their respective states,"[4] the electors are expressly forbidden from meeting as a national body.

This prohibition has prevented presidential electors from ever—*even once*—playing a deliberative role in the selection of the president.

Instead, with very few exceptions, presidential electors have followed the popular election results.

Even in the very first presidential election, presidential electors did not exercise independent judgment to choose the president *or* the vice president.

George Washington was the "consensus candidate" for the presidency even while the Constitution was being written. He won the electoral vote unanimously—the only president ever to have done so.

But it can't be said that the presidential electors *selected* Washington; the choice was agreed upon well in advance and was not the result of their deliberations.

Similarly, in the first election, John Adams was the consensus candidate for the vice presidency.

Adams led the field by a large margin and won easily, even though the electoral vote for the vice presidency was divided between eleven candidates.

This was because Adams was the de facto nominee of the Federalist Party.

Thus, even in the first election, presidential electors did not deliberately select the president *or* the vice president.

In other words, even in the first election, the Electoral College did not work the way the framers had envisioned. Thus we can say the Electoral College *never once* worked the way the framers had envisioned.

In addition, even the first election revealed the power of partisan nominations to influence the election result, even though the "nominations" were informal.

What history does not record is that the de facto nominations made in that first election prevented untold chaos from ensuing.

The first election suggests the advantage (and perhaps even the necessity) of party nomination, to consolidate support behind a few carefully chosen candidates.

* * *

By the time Washington announced his retirement in 1796, the actual workings of the Electoral College were clear to anyone who cared to observe.

The reality was that any group able to consolidate a coalition behind one candidate would have a huge advantage in the Electoral College.

In 1796, the Democratic-Republicans in Congress agreed to support Thomas Jefferson for president. The Federalists agreed to support John Adams.

The congressional caucus of each faction made its nomination. The caucuses were held in secret to avoid scrutiny. It was well understood that the nominees would gain a huge advantage from a closed, cliquish process that was not provided by the Constitution.

After the election was over, and the electoral vote tallied, Adams had won the presidency.

In an interesting twist, however, Jefferson—his erstwhile opponent—had won the vice presidency.

The outcome was the result of a quirk in the original Electoral College, which awarded the vice presidency to the second largest winner of the electoral vote.

The result of the election was the first—and only—divided presidential administration in American history.

The election of 1796 thus showcased the effectiveness of party nominations, but also revealed a serious defect in the original Electoral College.

Again in 1800, the same defect was a major factor in the outcome of the election.

In 1800, Jefferson tied in the electoral vote with his vice presidential running mate Aaron Burr, who then proceeded to try to steal the election.

When the election was cast into the House, Jefferson nearly lost. It took thirty-six ballots and a conspiracy for Jefferson to finally prevail over Burr.

The result spurred a movement to reform the Electoral College via constitutional amendment. This led directly to the passage of Twelfth Amendment, which altered the method of balloting in the Electoral College.

In the original Electoral College, the first-place winner of the electoral vote won the presidency and the second-place winner won the vice presidency.

Under the Twelfth Amendment, electoral votes for the president and vice president are cast on distinct ballots. This was intended to allow presidential and vice presidential candidates to tie in the electoral vote without triggering a contingency election in the House.

This change to the Electoral College had the effect of legitimizing party nominations for the presidency and vice presidency.

Prior to the Twelfth Amendment, the advantage of a partisan nomination could be negated if the election was ultimately decided by the House.

The Twelfth Amendment thus paved the way for the development of presidential nominating procedures within the political parties.

Modeled after the legislative caucuses in use at the state level, the congressional caucus system was the first mode of nomination to fill the opening created by the Twelfth Amendment.[5]

The congressional caucuses of each party convened during presidential election years to choose the parties' nominees; the nominees were then announced to the states through committees of correspondence.[6]

The caucus system served a vital function even though it was an improvised practice; but the system also had a number of flaws that would make it short-lived.

The caucus system secured an orderly succession to the presidency, but it did so at the expense of popular control and electoral accountability.

During the heyday of the caucus system, between 1809 and 1829, no president was elected who hadn't first served as secretary of state under the prior two-term president. Whether this was due to rigidity or wisdom is hard to say. In any case, this custom was followed during the entire time the caucus system remained in use.

The inflexibility of the system was also revealed in the "Virginia Dynasty" of 1801 to 1825, during which time every president originated from Virginia.

While many reasons factored into Virginia's dominance, the rigid and non-deliberative character of the caucus system was certainly among those reasons.

The caucus system also gave rise to a kind of one-party rule at the national level. This was brought about by the Democratic-Republican Party's long-term control of Congress,[7] which gave the party a monopoly over the only legitimate means of presidential nomination.

Lastly, the caucus system weakened presidential power vis-à-vis Congress by increasing Congress's sway over cabinet officers who harbored presidential ambitions.

Although it was a worthy first attempt at forging a nominating process, the caucus system was riddled with inherent defects that would soon lead to its demise.

* * *

By the election of 1824, the congressional caucus system was on the verge of failure.

Although President James Monroe won reelection easily in 1820—he won all but one electoral vote—the caucus had nothing to do with the result because it wasn't convened that year.[8]

The apparent tranquility of the 1820 election masked the deeper currents that were eroding the legitimacy and foundation of the congressional caucus system.

In 1824, the caucus met with just sixty-six members of Congress present; and most hailed from just four states.

In addition, it *just so happened* that nearly every member of the caucus supported Treasury Secretary William Crawford in his bid for the presidency.

Although Crawford duly won the caucus's nomination, he proceeded to place fourth in a four-way popular vote for the presidency.

The election of 1824 was also Andrew Jackson's first run for the presidency.

Jackson might have won the race, had he the benefit of a national party nomination.

Even without a party nomination, Jackson won the popular vote *and* the electoral vote. He just didn't win the majority in the Electoral College needed to avoid a contingency election in the House.

After the election was cast into the House, the "intrigue & cabal"[9] that characterized the congressional selection of presidents since 1800 kicked into high gear.

Under the Twelfth Amendment, the House would consider only the top three winners of the electoral vote. This meant that Speaker of the House Henry Clay was not eligible for consideration. Clay was nonetheless in a prime position to influence the vote; and charges of corruption flew even before the vote was taken.

The supreme irony of the House's decision was that it caused yet another secretary of state—this time, John Quincy Adams—to be elected to the presidency. Upon reaching the presidency, Adams repaid Clay by appointing Clay as *his* secretary of state. Under the prevailing custom of the day, Clay was now in line for a preordained succession to the presidency. But, as history attests, Clay's rise to the presidency never happened.

Jackson denounced the "corrupt bargain" that had taken place; and his supporters immediately set to work dismantling and replacing the failed caucus system.

* * *

After the election of 1828, the Jacksonians wasted no time in organizing the system that would carry Andrew Jackson to victory in the following election.

The device they conceived was the party convention system; but the convention system they formed did not spring up overnight.

States like Pennsylvania and Massachusetts had used party conventions to nominate, even in the 1790s.[10] Although practices varied by party and by election, these states were known to use party conventions instead of the legislative caucus.

The big problem with the caucus system was that it left a legislative district unrepresented if the district happened to be represented by the opposite party in the legislature.

Democratic-Republicans in New York tried to remedy this problem in 1817 by convening the state's first "mixed caucus."[11] As in the pure caucus system, elected lawmakers held most seats. But there were also a large contingent of delegates elected by Democratic-Republican voters of districts held by the opposite party.

Although the mixed caucus better represented the people than the pure caucus system, it fell short of the popular control offered by the party convention system.

These early nominating practices in New York are significant from a national standpoint not only because they were innovative. They were also the practices that informed Martin Van Buren's early political education.

Van Buren, who would later succeed Jackson as president, was the mastermind who organized the party conventions that secured Jackson's victory in 1828.

The party convention system cobbled together after the 1824 election was an assortment of state conventions, mass meetings, and even state legislative endorsements.[12]

These assemblies proclaimed their support for Jackson and bolstered his candidacy; but the process did not result in a nomination, because no national nominating assembly was convened in 1828.

Van Buren's associates are said to have worried about factional strife within the fledgling party, which would have undermined Jackson's candidacy. For that reason, they did not wish to risk holding a national convention.[13]

And so the party convention system that swept Jackson into office was not only novel, but provisional as well; it was not fully developed in time for the election.

In fact, the Jacksonian Democrats were not even the first party to hold a *national* convention. The first national convention was held by the Anti-Mason Party in September of 1831.[14]

The party convention system was not firmly established even after the Democrats held *their* first national convention in 1832—a convention that renominated Jackson unanimously.

In the very next election of 1836, the Whig Party opted to nominate four regional candidates instead of holding a national convention.

The Whig strategy was to win enough electoral votes to deny victory to the Democratic nominee, then unify behind one candidate after the election was cast into the House. The strategy was a disaster and was not repeated.

The election of 1836 proved that any party seeking to win the presidency needs to hold a national convention; and no major party has failed to do so since.

* * *

The party convention system overtook other nominating methods because the system offered advantages no party could afford to be without.

The party convention system served a number of important functions:

- It consolidated the voting strength of the party behind a single, unified ticket.

- It fostered coalition-building between diverse sectional and ideological factions.

- It vetted and selected candidates who were moderate in temper and appeal.

- It removed nominations from legislative control, thus reinforcing the separation of powers.

- It upheld the representative principle at the heart of our republican form of government.

- It allowed for real popular participation and control in the nominating process.

- And, it allowed the parties to formulate their platform and then select candidates accordingly.

At the grassroots of the party convention system were the primary assemblies—what we would call precinct conventions (or caucuses)—run by local party members in rural towns and urban neighborhoods.

At the precinct conventions, party members would (and still do) vote for the first round of secondary convention delegates, either by voice vote or by ballot.[15]

The delegates chosen at the precinct level would then attend the party's county convention, its congressional district convention, or both.[16] These conventions would nominate candidates to offices within their jurisdiction and also chose delegates to the state party convention.

State conventions would assemble to nominate candidates for statewide office and also select delegates to represent the state party at the national convention.

The intricate structure of the convention system formed an independent, vital ladder from the lowest to the highest offices of government.

The organization of the party convention system not only *mirrored*, but also served to *fortify*, federalism.

In addition, the party convention system held the separation of powers intact, during the era while party conventions were empowered to select candidates.

The system also held ambitious office-seekers in check by removing many factors in the nominating process from the immediate control of candidates.

Following its idyllic early years, however, the convention system was gradually corrupted, especially during the latter half of the nineteenth century.

The corruption began in the local precinct caucuses, especially in urban precincts, and spread upward.

CARL JARVIS

The abuses included stuffed ballot boxes, fistfights, illegal voters, and "snap" caucuses to prevent most voters from attending the caucus in the first place. These abuses were often intended to secure control of convention delegates and thus control of conventions and nominations. As abuses in the precinct conventions became a serious problem, states began to regulate the primary process under law.

In the 1890s, many states passed primary election laws to ensure the integrity of the primary process. The laws ensured free and fair elections for delegates and provided judicial recourse for enforcement. The laws served to strengthen the party convention system.

Unfortunately, however, the primary election laws did not address an emerging problem within the party convention system: credentials disputes.

Credentials are the documents delegates receive to certify their membership in the convention assembly, which then allows them to vote on convention business.

Credentials disputes are used, even today, to challenge the seating of duly-elected delegates at conventions. Credentials disputes become especially heated when one faction tries to use the adjudication process to wrest control of the convention from another.

As Fredrick Dallinger recounted of one dispute in New York, "Duly-elected delegates were unhesitatingly unseated, and their seats given to contesting delegations composed of faithful adherents of the machine."[17]

In response to such abuses, states began to regulate conventions under state law similar to the way they'd begun to regulate the primary process.

It was not long, however, before gradual reforms to the party convention system were abandoned, in favor of reforms that would abolish the system altogether.

The shift in the reformers' focus was subtle. In general, direct primary reformers did not openly declare war on the party convention system.

Rather, they presented direct primary reform in terms of a false but alluring comparison between primary elections and general elections, even though the two were never meant to be the same.

Direct primary reformers began to insist that ensuring the integrity of primary elections was *not enough*.

They argued that, in addition to ensuring the integrity of primary elections, candidates' names had to replace delegates' names on the primary ballot.

It's obvious that this reform had nothing to do with ensuring the integrity of primary elections, which is where the major abuses were occurring.

If that was the intent, then placing candidates' names on the ballot was beside the point.

The real intent—*whether conscious or not*—was to undermine the representative character of the party convention system.

It's also worth noting that putting candidates' names on the ballot in lieu of delegates' names did not alleviate the main problem in the conventions either.

In fact, it made the problem *worse*.

The problem in the conventions was the lack of an acceptable process for adjudicating credentials disputes.

The theory was that direct primaries would reduce credentials disputes by binding delegates to particular candidates in advance of the conventions.

Instead, the opposite happened: the direct primary actually caused credentials disputes *to explode*.

The reason was simple: the direct primary made conventions into no-holds-barred battles between candidate-centered factions of pledged delegates.

The 1972 Democratic National Convention, for example, had the largest number of credentials disputes of any national convention in American history.[18] The irony is that this was also the first convention in which a majority of delegates were pledged to candidates via direct primary.

Credentials disputes would continue to be a problem even today, for the Democratic Party, except the Party then adopted a rule to allow candidates to vet and slate their own pledged delegates.

Modern party conventions in which no deliberations take place are thus creatures of the direct primary system, because so many delegates are pledged to candidates in advance via direct primary.

* * *

The subtle change to the primary ballot may *seem* inconsequential, even looking back on it today.

It may *seem* like a minor modification to the primary election laws.

But even the actual changes to state law reflect an awareness of the nature of the change.

This awareness is reflected in the distinction that was maintained between presidential primaries and primaries for all other federal, state, and local offices.

Before we get to that, though, it's important to highlight the difference between direct and indirect primary election.

Direct primaries are also called *candidate preference* primaries. In a direct primary, the candidate's name appears on the primary ballot; convention delegate's names are usually not on the ballot.

Indirect primaries are also known as *delegate selection* primaries. In an indirect primary, the voter is electing a delegate to represent them at the party convention.

It's important to note this subtle distinction because it was maintained in the presidential nominating process, *even after most other offices were brought under the direct primary system.*

In other words, even while direct primary reform was sweeping the country, true believers stopped short of pressing for direct primaries in the presidential nominating process.

In 1901, Florida enacted an optional direct primary law that applied to state and congressional offices, including U.S. senators. But the law allowed presidential primaries only to the extent of "Nominating Delegates to Political Conventions." That is, no presidential direct primary was authorized under the original Florida law.[19]

In 1905, Wisconsin passed a mandatory primary law that applied to the selection of national convention delegates. But the law did not allow or require a candidate preference vote.[20]

In 1906, Pennsylvania was the first state to give potential delegates the option to list the candidates they would support, if selected to attend a convention.[21]

And in 1910, Oregon became the first state to establish a mandatory direct primary for the presidency, *requiring* primary voters to express candidate preference.[22] Other states would soon follow in requiring presidential candidates' names to appear on the primary ballot.[23]

The election of 1912 was thus the first to involve the use of the presidential direct primary.

Theodore Roosevelt had already served two terms as president. Although he was ineligible under the two-term tradition, Roosevelt entered and won nine of the twelve presidential primaries held that year.

At the Republican National Convention, Roosevelt used his primary victories to claim a mandate to the nomination, even though he controlled only 278 out of 1078 delegates.

The Convention rejected Roosevelt's flimsy claim to the nomination and instead renominated sitting President William Howard Taft, as it was likely to have done in any case, had Roosevelt not entered the race.

Furious at the result, Roosevelt bolted the party and became the presidential nominee of the Bull Moose-Progressive Party.

Roosevelt's third-party candidacy split the Republican vote; and the division within the party can be largely attributed to the uneven adoption and distinct effects of the presidential direct primary.

The split within the Republican Party allowed New Jersey Governor Woodrow Wilson to be elected to the presidency, essentially without a contest.

Wilson thus became the first president elected due to the influence of the presidential direct primary system.

Although only a small number of presidential direct primaries were held in 1912, the effects of the presidential direct primary already far exceeded its strength on the basis of delegates alone.

* * *

Between 1912 and 1916, the number of "presidential primary" states grew from twelve to twenty.[24]

Although the increase would seem to have expanded the influence of the direct primary, the meaning of "presidential primary" needs careful definition to see what was really happening.

In many of the new "presidential primary" states, the practice of selecting delegates did not materially change.

In 1920, for example, presidential primary states like New Hampshire, New York, and Massachusetts did not hold candidate preference elections for the presidency.[25]

Instead, these states sent uncommitted delegates to the Democratic and Republican National Conventions.

In terms of percentage, 58% of Republican National Convention delegates were selected by primary; but only around 35% were pledged to a particular candidate.

Despite their small share of the total, pledged delegates had enormous influence on the Convention outcome.

Let's ponder for a moment that the phrase "smoke-filled room" entered the American political lexicon during the 1920 election,[26] just as the deliberative party convention system was dying a quiet death.

The insinuation is that President Warren Harding's scandal-ridden administration was hatched in the backrooms of the Republican National Convention.

This suggestion is ironic since the decision of the Convention was so *largely determined in advance* by the direct primary vote.

If Warren Harding was nominated in a "smoke-filled room," he won the nomination because of the direct primary.

Harding entered the Convention with one of the largest blocks of pledged delegates of any candidate, mostly pledged via the Ohio presidential primary.

* * *

It's interesting to look back at efforts to *avoid* using the direct primary to nominate presidential candidates, especially when the direct primary was first adopted.

After 1920, the number of presidential primary states receded. Between 1920 and 1936, *eight states* repealed their presidential primary requirements.

During this period—and until 1972—the combination of direct and indirect primaries gave rise to the so-called "mixed convention" system of presidential nomination.

Under the mixed convention system, a combination of pledged delegates and uncommitted delegates were sent to the national conventions of both major parties.

Under the mixed system, pledged delegates usually limited the field of possible candidates, while uncommitted delegates ultimately chose the nominee.

Thus, under the mixed system, direct primaries had a persuasive but not controlling influence over the presidential nominating process of both parties.

This began to change during the 1960s as more states adopted presidential primaries. Between 1968 and 1972, the number of "presidential primary" states grew rapidly.

Unlike in the 1910s, however, states were enacting direct (rather than indirect) primary laws. Thus in this second wave of reform, an increasing share of delegates were pledged to candidates chosen by direct primary.

During the 1970s, this shift resulted in a complete transformation of the presidential nominating process.

Prior to 1972, early states like New Hampshire had a tiny influence over the presidential nominating process, because conventions still made the final selection.

In 1972, however, a critical threshold was crossed. For the first time in American history, a majority of delegates to both national conventions were pledged in advance to candidates chosen by direct primary.

This meant that a majority of delegates were bound to particular candidates before the conventions were ever called to order. As a result, convention proceedings were a foregone conclusion—in reality, if not in the alternate universe of media hype and spin.

In ways *still* not widely recognized today, this change to the nominating system revolutionized the American political process—and its rhetoric—from top to bottom.

* * *

Learning to see the history of the nominating process as the "secret thread" of American political history takes no great feat of imagination.

It demands only the recognition that the nominating process is the actual selection mechanism for nearly every elected office in the country.

Today, there's *overwhelming evidence* that primary elections matter far more than general elections in determining who actually gets elected.

But primary elections are even more important, because they don't just determine *who* gets elected.

They affect rotation in office as well as the distribution of power throughout our entire political system.

The direct primary, in particular, has had effects on our Constitution—especially in the last one hundred years—that most people can't conceptualize.

As we'll explore in far more detail, the direct primary is the single most important key to understanding how our political system was turned upside down, during a century when the Constitution changed hardly at all.

5

Rotation in Office and Entrenched Incumbency

Today elections in America are a one-way street.

An election may offer a degree of choice in an open seat race, but elections in general are not a practical way to remove incumbents from office.

The demise of electoral accountability can be observed from the presidency down to the state and local level.

Once elected, it is well near impossible for voters to turn an incumbent elected official out of office today.

And the problem is becoming worse every year.

The decline of rotation in office is divorcing incumbents from the constituents they purport to serve.

This problem of declining rotation in office has led many people to believe that term limits are the solution.

But terms limits deal only with the symptoms—at best—and they do *not* address the root of the problem.

Term limits may furnish the *appearance* of rotation in office, but they don't curb the advantages that allow elected officials to win reelection over and over.

Thus in many cases, term limits do *not* secure rotation in office *during the allowed period of service.*

To restore the true *spirit* of rotation in office, we must address the underlying institutional cause of entrenched incumbency.

∗ ∗ ∗

Over the twentieth century, the frequency of rotation in office declined in the United States.

As Matthew Glassman and Erin Hemlin observe of the House of Representatives:

> During the 20th century, the average years of service for Representatives steadily increased, from an average of just over four years in the first two Congresses of the century to an average of approximately 10 years in the three most recent Congresses.[1]

They similarly observe of the Senate that:

> Historically, the average years of service among Senators has been similar to that of Representatives, with little variation during the first 100 years after the founding, followed by a steady increase over the next 100 years...Average years of service peaked at 13.4 years of service in the 111th Congress (2009-2010).[2]

In attempting to explain this trend, it's important to note that the trend is not confined to Congress.

The trend is even more striking in the presidency, *even though we have presidential term limits.*

The purpose of rotation in office, after all, is not for elected officials to serve for a set number of years. The spirit of rotation in office is for citizens to have the power to remove incumbents from office *in the course of any given election.*

Since the early twentieth century, however, the power of ordinary citizens to remove incumbents from office has diminished, along with electoral turnover.

If we want to strike at the heart of the problem, term limits are not enough.

But to determine what to do, first we need to understand *why* rotation in office is plummeting in virtually every elected office in the country.

* * *

The history of the presidency not only chronicles the demise of rotation in office, but it is also a history that is well documented and widely known.[3]

It's worth noting a few facts about rotation in office in the presidency right at the outset.

Before 1910, no president was allowed to run for a third term; and several presidents were denied renomination even to *second* term—an occurrence that would be unimaginable today.

Since 1910, we've had two presidents nominated to third terms. We've even had one nominated to a fourth term. Meanwhile, *no president who sought a second term has been denied renomination since 1910.*

To see where we *are* with respect to rotation in office in the presidency, it's crucial to know where we've *been*.

George Washington established the two-term tradition when he left the presidency voluntarily after serving for eight years. The precedent set by Washington prevailed uninterrupted for over a century.

Although Washington was selfless in establishing the two-term tradition, the tradition was *not* maintained *voluntarily* by everyone who followed him in office.

In 1880, Ulysses Grant, who had already served for two terms, allowed his name to be floated as a possible third-term candidate. Under today's presidential direct primary system (and without presidential term limits), Grant may have won renomination purely due to name recognition. But under the party convention system, Grant's supporters failed to secure enough delegates and his bid for renomination quietly died.

In 1896, Grover Cleveland sought a third term. This instance was even more dramatic since Cleveland was a sitting president, vested with the powers of office. Under today's system, it's hard to imagine Cleveland *not* winning renomination. Under the existing system, not only was Cleveland denied renomination; the party rebuked him, declaring that "no man should be eligible for a third term of the Presidential office."[4]

In each case when the two-term tradition was challenged prior to 1910, it was upheld by the national party conventions even in the absence of formal, constitutional term limits.

The party convention system was even more impressive in its power and ability to deny renomination to sitting presidents.

Denial of renomination to sitting presidents has occurred only four times in the history of our country, and every instance took place *before* 1910.

In 1844, John Tyler had become so unpopular with members of his own Whig Party that the Whigs denied his reelection ambitions, by denying his renomination at the Whig National Convention.

In 1856, the Democrats for similar reasons denied Franklin Pierce's renomination.

In 1884, the Republican Party denied Chester Arthur renomination to a second term. Arthur had become president after James Garfield's assassination in 1881.

Finally, in 1896—in the instance already mentioned—the Democratic Party denied Grover Cleveland's renomination. This was perhaps due to Cleveland's unpopularity, but the stated reason was to uphold the two-term tradition.

With this record in mind, it is at least a point of curiosity as to why *not one sitting president* who sought reelection has been denied renomination since 1910.

This suggests that the national party convention system not only enforced the two-term tradition, but also denied advantage to incumbents and enforced rotation in office in a general sense as well.

* * *

As the party convention system was abandoned, the enforcement of the two-term tradition faltered as well, beginning in the 1912 election.

In 1908, Theodore Roosevelt had declined to seek a third term as president, citing "the wise custom which limited the President to two terms."[5]

By 1912, however, with ambition corrupting his judgment, Roosevelt had a change of heart. He threw his "[hat] in the ring"[6]—as he said—against President William Howard Taft, even though he'd personally endorsed Taft as his successor just four years earlier.

Roosevelt entered and won nine of the twelve primaries held that year, this being the first election in which the presidential direct primary was used.

At the Republican National Convention, Roosevelt's questionable claim to the nomination was rejected.

Roosevelt stormed out and instead became the presidential nominee of the Bull Moose-Progressive Party, just a few weeks later.

Thus Roosevelt became the first two-term president nominated to a third term, albeit by a third party.[7]

Roosevelt's run for a third term in 1912 revealed a crack in the integrity of the two-term tradition that his cousin, Franklin Roosevelt, would fully exploit in 1940.

While Franklin Roosevelt was quiet about his ambition to run for a third term, his renomination was all but assured when he allowed his name to appear on the primary ballot of every state that held a primary that year. Roosevelt became the presumptive nominee in 1940 well before the National Convention was held.

In similar fashion, Roosevelt overrode all prior custom in 1944, when he was renominated to an unprecedented *fourth* term. Roosevelt held the office until he died of poor health just a few months after his reelection.

Roosevelt's ambition to remain in office indefinitely—and his party's unwillingness or inability to prevent him from doing so—became the main reason for the passage of the Twenty-Second Amendment in 1951.

The Twenty-Second Amendment provides "no person shall be elected to the office of the President more than twice," and details the rules in case of a partial first term.

The Twenty-Second Amendment made the unwritten two-term tradition into a formal constitutional mandate.

But the question whether constitutional term limits have effectively secured the *spirit* of rotation in office—*especially in recent decades*—is a question that deserves far greater attention than it has received.

* * *

If the history of the presidency demonstrates the decline of rotation in office, the same trend can be observed in the vice presidency as well.

Before 1910, *not one* sitting vice president was ever renominated to a second term by a national convention.[8]

Since 1910, the renomination of vice presidential incumbents has been the rule, barring just two exceptions.

Also since 1910, presidents have exercised far more control over the choice of their vice presidential running mates—including the decision whether to renominate—than would have been imaginable prior to 1910.

Going back to the 1830s—when the national convention system was first established—the unwritten rule was for vice presidents to leave office after one term.

The reason had to do with the desire of each party to balance its ticket ideologically and geographically, the use of the office as a spoil for quelling factionalism, and a prevailing belief in the principle of rotation in office.

To manage these demands, the vice presidential selection was made by the national party conventions—and *not*, as it is today, by presidents and presidential nominees.

In contrast to the era *before* 1910, only a few incumbent vice presidents have been denied renomination to a second term *since* 1910.

Even in 1912, Vice President James Sherman was renominated despite the well-known fact that he was in failing health. His health was so bad that he died before the election.

Sherman's renomination may have been intended to show a unified face against Roosevelt's insurgency that year. Whatever may have been the motive, however, the renomination was not only ill conceived, but also unprecedented at the time.

As renomination of incumbent vice presidents has been the rule since 1910, this makes the exceptions all the more noteworthy.

There have been only two.

In 1944, during Roosevelt's fourth-term bid, the Democratic Party rejected Vice President Henry Wallace's renomination to a second term. Had he been renominated, Wallace would have been the first to succeed to the presidency upon Roosevelt's death in April of 1945. With Roosevelt in poor health, party leaders moved to prevent Wallace's candidacy.

The 1944 Democratic National Convention thus became *among the last* national conventions in which party leaders and delegates selected the vice president. At the same time, Henry Wallace became *the very last* sitting vice president to be denied renomination to a second term by a national convention.

Since then, it's been customary for the president (or presidential nominee) to make the selection. Because of the way denial of renomination would be perceived, presidents have no incentive to ensure rotation in office.

In 1976, Nelson Rockefeller became the only other incumbent vice president, since 1910, not to be renominated to a second term alongside the incumbent president.

But the situation with Rockefeller was different than with Wallace. Rockefeller had been appointed rather than elected, and he apparently made the decision himself not to seek renomination.

* * *

It's tempting to view the decline of rotation in office over the past one hundred years in oversimplified terms.

Gerrymandering is often taken to be the main reason for the rise of entrenched incumbency.

While gerrymandering today is indeed worse than ever,[9] there are two major problems with depicting gerrymandering as the root of entrenched incumbency.[10]

First, gerrymandering is nothing new. Although the practice has evolved, gerrymandering has existed since before the Constitution was formed.

Second, gerrymandering does not account for the rise of entrenched incumbency in the presidency, vice presidency, or U.S. Senate.

For that matter, gerrymandering does not account for the rise of entrenched incumbency in the state and local offices for which there are no districts *or* redistricting.

Since the decline of rotation in office can be observed across all branches of government—*and at all levels*—this suggests that we need to look deeper to find the real root of entrenched incumbency.

* * *

The entrenched incumbency we see today stems from the very same factors that give incumbents a degree of advantage *at all times* and *under all possible systems*.

First, incumbents can raise money far more easily than their challengers.

Second, incumbents typically enjoy greater name recognition than their challengers.

Third, incumbents have a controlling influence over the political conversation at any given time. This includes control over *which* issues are discussed, *how* those issues are discussed (especially their appeal to specific constituencies), and *when* those issues are discussed (especially with respect to the election cycle).

Although these factors are *always* an advantage to incumbents, the degree of that advantage depends on the mode of nomination in use.

To understand the effects of the mode of nomination on incumbency advantage, it helps to view the major nominating systems we've used—the party convention system and the direct primary—in comparative terms.

To evaluate the party convention system against the direct primary, we might ask the following questions:

- First: under each system, how much money do candidates need to win nomination? Who raises the funds; and who controls the funds—the candidate or the party?

- Second: under each system, how much influence does name recognition have on the nominating decision? To what extent does the media influence the "anointing" of candidates?

- Lastly: under each system, to what degree do candidates control the appeals they make and the issues they emphasize? To what degree does the party manage or control political messaging?

These questions evaluate the performance of different nominating systems, and the effects those systems have on incumbency advantage.

Given the effects of the direct primary on each of these factors, it's clear the direct primary had *something* to do with the decline in rotation in office since 1910.

There are several connections between direct primaries and entrenched incumbency: the amount of money direct primaries require, the name recognition advantage they confer, and the candidate control over messaging and issue selection they allow.

Each effect of the direct primary stands in contrast to the effects of the party convention system.

* * *

First, let's look at the money direct primaries require.

Direct primaries require candidates to raise an enormous amount of money just to win nomination.

The amount of money can range from a million dollars for a contested House seat, to several million for a Senate seat, to tens of millions for the presidency.

The fundraising burden alone causes many primaries to go uncontested.

Even when primaries *are* contested, there is often a lack of credible candidates, and it's well-known that campaign contributors tend to favor incumbents.

Campaign finance laws and contribution limits further skew the money advantage in favor of incumbents.

Aside from the incumbency advantage attributable to money, the direct primary forces candidates to raise the money themselves, since the parties afford no aid in the nominating process.

Not only does this place candidates directly under obligation to their campaign contributors; it also requires candidates to exercise direct control over their own campaign funds, so that the money is spent *entirely* at their discretion—including on lobbying their former colleagues after they leave office.

In summary, the amount of money it takes to win nomination by direct primary serves to entrench incumbents, who are simply better positioned to raise the enormous sums needed.

＊ ＊ ＊

Second, let's look at the effects of name recognition in direct primaries.

Direct primaries give candidates with prior name recognition a huge advantage.

This effect tends to favor incumbents, celebrities, or those with a famous family name, political name, or both. Increasingly, candidates are selected on the basis of name recognition, and *not* on the basis of their record of prior service.

In most contested primaries, name recognition will give incumbents a decisive advantage over a less-known challenger.

The name recognition advantage is so powerful that it even affects the type of candidate that's viable in the first place. Since the advent of the direct primary, the system has yielded many so-called "mini-royal"[11] dynasties.

Examples include the LaFollette dynasty in Wisconsin and the Kennedy dynasty in the Northeast. Examples also include the Bush presidential dynasty and the near-rise of a Clinton dynasty (perhaps soon to be revived).

These are only the most well-known examples. Many other examples are found at the state and local level. Political dynasties large and small have multiplied since the adoption of the direct primary, and *they did not exist under the party convention system.*[12]

The rise of political dynasties demonstrates—at an extreme—the potential danger of the name recognition advantage conferred by direct primary elections.

The name recognition advantage offered by direct primaries is so powerful that it has real implications for term limits reform.

There are many examples—some famous, some not-so-famous—of candidates bypassing term limits, and other bans against running for office, by running family members in their place.

In 1917, Governor James "Pa" Ferguson of Texas was impeached and banned for life from holding office in the state. To bypass the ban, he ran his wife "Ma" Ferguson as a surrogate candidate for governor. She won and became caretaker of the office while he ran the state.[13] The Fergusons are well known because the Clintons later adopted their campaign slogan—"two for the price of one"—when Bill ran for the presidency in 1992.

In 1966, Governor George Wallace of Alabama ran up against the state's gubernatorial term limits. To skirt the term limits, he ran his wife Lurleen as "Mrs. George C. Wallace." Lurleen Wallace won, and George Wallace ran the state for a partial term until she died.[14] Wallace's story is well known because a few years later he became a controversial third-party candidate for president.

Especially in states that have legislative term limits, "mini-royal" dynasties are rampant today: one family member is barred from running for reelection due to term limits, so they look around the kitchen table to find a wife, son, or other relative to succeed them in office.[15]

While dynastic nepotism may comply with the letter of the law, it is contrary to the *spirit* of rotation in office and the *intent* of term limits reform.

Aside from the issue of nepotism, these examples illustrate the futility of securing *true* rotation in office under the direct primary. This is because, once elected, the mini-royals bring with them the same courtiers and retainers who previously served other family members.

To summarize: the fundraising and name recognition advantages offered by the direct primary serve to entrench incumbents in elected office.

* * *

Third, let's look at the candidate control of messaging and issue selection that direct primaries allow.

Direct primaries place candidates in control of every appeal they make. Candidates are free to disregard the resolutions of the party platform not only during their primary campaign—*but also during their term of office.*

In practical terms, this means that candidates say and do whatever they feel is necessary to win nomination.

This gives special advantage to deceitful or demagogic candidates.

Candidates can take any stance and beat the drum on any issue—no matter how inflammatory, imprudent, or injurious—and no one can intervene, whether for the good of the country or even for the welfare of the party.

Candidates can lie, make empty promises, or speak in meaningless generalities; and there's no one in a position to hold candidates accountable for bizarre behavior.

On top of that, direct primaries actually give candidates the *incentive* to arouse base emotions in order to sway the *tiny segment of the electorate* whose support the candidate needs to win nomination.

This is why primary election appeals are often unrelated to the serious issues facing the country. Once elected, these same appeals drive the priorities and agenda of elected officials.

Candidate control of issue selection not only sidelines the role of the parties as intermediaries, but also allows candidates to "set the agenda" of the nation's political conversation around the most irresponsible and self-serving issues imaginable.

Once in the bully pulpit of office, candidates ply the same emotional appeals and rhetoric they used to win nomination to remain in office indefinitely.

* * *

In recent decades, with the fall and decline of the parties as meaningful intermediaries—mainly due to the effects of the direct primary—incumbency advantage has skyrocketed.

The effects have become so extreme that incumbency advantage stands at unprecedented levels today.

All of the effects detailed so far—money, name recognition, and issue selection—assume the existence of *contested* direct primary elections, which are fewer and ever diminishing in number.

Most primaries are won today by an incumbent in the absence of a primary challenger.

Within the universe of *contested* primaries, there are very few in which the challenger stands any chance of winning.

All of these effects are magnified in the case of the presidency so that many states *no longer even bother to hold* presidential primaries for the incumbent party.

The cancellation of presidential primaries in various states began in 1984, and the practice has only become more common since then.

Look at the presidential primary record from the 2004 or 2012 presidential cycles, and you'll find a number of states that simply did not hold an incumbent presidential primary.

Of course, why hold a presidential primary when no challenger of an incumbent president can realistically win anyway?

This question, along with the cancellation of primaries, gets to the very heart of everything wrong with the direct primary system we use today.

The cancellation of primaries is certainly among the most disturbing developments to transpire since the direct primary system was first adopted.

The cancellation of primaries is disturbing because it reveals the tendencies of the direct primary system at an extreme which is becoming commonplace.

It is ironic that the cancellation of presidential primaries began after the 1980 election, which was the election when Jimmy Carter was renominated against the wishes of his party. His renomination was all but assured when he entered the primaries. Carter won the primaries—and the nomination at the convention—with little real contest. Despite his renomination, Carter's attitude toward his own party ensured that he would lose the election that followed.[16]

The 1980 election thus quietly marked the triumph of the direct primary in presidential politics. Jimmy Carter is precisely the type who would *not* have been renominated under the party convention system, for the sake of the party's prospects if for no other reason.

* * *

What if the party convention system was actually the best system we ever had, for ensuring rotation in office and minimizing incumbency advantage?

I believe it was, for three main reasons.

First, party conventions did not specially favor candidates with prodigious fundraising abilities.

The reason was simple: candidates did not have to raise large amounts of money (or really any money at all) to win nomination. Also, the expense of holding the conventions (which was minor in contrast to the expense of a primary campaign) was borne by the parties, which prevented candidates from having to control the funds.

Second, party conventions did not necessarily favor candidates with name recognition.

The conventions tended to go deeper into the field of available candidates to select so-called "dark horse" candidates. These candidates were often either unknown or seemingly not in the running for nomination, yet they were exceptionally well qualified in most cases.

Third, party conventions kept candidates' appeals tempered and in check.

The party convention system was guided by the principle of "measures before men." Candidates were selected by conventions to carry out the party's agenda; party doctrines were *not* placed at the mercy of candidates willing to say anything in order to win nomination. Party conventions left almost no latitude for candidates to engage in base emotional appeals.

The party convention system thus moderated the behavior of candidates and kept the incumbency advantage of elected officials in check.

Every effect of the party convention system conspired to ensure rotation in office, much in contrast to the direct primary system we use today.

* * *

Today, even as the effects of the direct primary system are plainly evident before our eyes, the effects are not often recognized as such.

There's great confusion in the way we often discuss the nominating system we use today.

The direct primary is often said to be "democratic," and the party convention system "undemocratic."

But setting aside abstract theory, the tendencies of each system are the opposite of what is often supposed.

Under the party convention system, a nomination was not decided by the amount of money the candidate raised, by the family name or pedigree of the candidate, or by the selfishly demagogic appeals made by the candidate. Today, under the direct primary, these are all factors that determine the outcome of nominating races.

The genius of the party convention system was that it did *not* leave our system exposed to the unseemly ambition of candidates. Rather, it limited the power of candidates by restraining their latitude, initiative, and role within the nominating process.

Under the party convention system, the parties decided nominations for the good of the country and for the good of the party as well. A candidate's selfish desire for office was of no account whatsoever.

Since the candidates' ambition had no weight in tipping the scales, the party convention system tended to produce candidates of an entirely different temperament and cast of mind than what we see today.

* * *

The vital question we now face is whether our liberties can much longer withstand the kind of limitless ambition it takes for candidates to win high office in the United States today.

Today, due to the sheer spectacle of the presidential nominating process, the process itself disqualifies any candidate who exhibits the slightest degree of modesty.

Meanwhile, we can't restore rule of law under leaders who are in love with their own delusions of grandeur.

Under the direct primary, candidates have too much latitude to determine their own messaging and conduct.

Once elected, latitude in the pursuit of office becomes latitude to ignore rule of law and trample civil liberties.

Even worse, the direct primary offers no real way to remove demagogues from office once they're in office.

As our entire political system gravitates further toward extremes, the direct primary *seems* to be the problem.

As direct primary elections do increasing damage with each election cycle, we face a stark choice.

We can go on *hoping* for that elusive "great leader" that we might *elect by direct primary,* or we can restore checks and balances to our nominating process.

In the final analysis, we cannot do both.

6

Distribution and Concentration of Power

Today presidential power is out of control, while Congress—meant to serve as a counterbalance—does little to restrain the scope of the executive power.[1]

Even more remarkably, uncontrolled presidential power has arisen over the past one hundred years, while the Constitution itself remained relatively unchanged.

Under the theory of the original Constitution, the branches of government were supposed to be checked and balanced against one another.

Madison expressed the philosophy behind the checks and balances with his famous maxim in *Federalist* no. 51: "Ambition must be made to counteract ambition."[2]

Today, however, we have regulatory czars who the Senate has not vetted or confirmed; we have a White House staff accountable to *no one* but the president; and we have a bureaucracy subject *only* to orders from on high (and not bound by any semblance of rule of law).

These conditions have yielded a concentration of power so great that the abuse of power has become not just *probable*, but increasingly *inevitable*.

Under the original Constitution, the liberty of the people was made to flourish in the crossfire between competing centers of power. This was to prevent political leaders from accumulating such power that they could run over ordinary citizens with impunity.

Yet today, many people disdain the checks and balances created by the framers of our Constitution; and our republican institutions are crumbling as a result.

* * *

The 1912 election marks a dividing line in American political history. Since that time, presidential power has steadily grown, largely at the expense of Congress.

In contrast to entrenched incumbency, the trend in the distribution of power is hard to quantify, but the change over the past century can be plainly observed.

Beginning in 1912, the power of the presidency began to grow rapidly. Although Congress has also asserted increasingly broad powers, many of its legislative acts have served to enhance the executive power.

Also beginning in 1912, the federal government's power began to increase relative to the states'.

Today, federal power eclipses state power.

These trends have resulted in a concentration of power so tightly bent around the *person* of the president that presidential power poses a serious threat to our republican form of government.

To stand any chance of reversing this concentration of power, we need to clearly understand the reason why it developed in the first place.

Many theories are offered, but the reality is quite simple: the skewed concentration of power we see today resulted from the *dissolution of intermediary powers.*

Today, the intermediaries that once prevented central authorities from amassing undue power *no longer exist.*

In *Federalist* no. 44, James Madison argued that state legislatures would be more liable to unconstitutional acts than Congress, due to the lack of intermediary powers between the legislatures and the people. He asserted that:

> There being no…intermediate body between the state legislature and the people, *interested in watching the conduct* of the [legislature], violations of the state constitutions are more likely…[3]

What did Madison mean by "intermediate body?" And how has this concept developed over time?

In the 1830s, Alexis de Tocqueville wrote:

> In Europe everything seems to conduce to the indefinite extension of the prerogatives of government…[because] the state tolerates no intermediate agent [or 'intermediary power'] between itself and the people.[4]

It is a well-known doctrine of our Constitution that power is restrained through checks and balances between the branches, which are assumed to yield a *separation* of powers and a *balance* of power.

It is a less-known doctrine, but an observation of both Madison and Tocqueville, that intermediary bodies are also an essential restraint on the power of government.

In fact, intermediary powers are possibly more important than constitutional checks and balances, as traditionally understood.

This aspect of the framers' carefully-conceived design is often overlooked; their method of providing intermediary powers was through the mode of election.[5]

Today, we'd also consider the mode of nomination—an aspect of our system that was unknown to them—as a means of establishing intermediary powers within the political process.

It is a common misconception that the framers established intermediary powers, via the indirect mode of election, to thwart the will of the people.

In fact, the framers viewed the indirect mode of election—and the resulting institutionalization of intermediary powers—as the best way to protect the people from demagogues who might contend for office from time to time.

The framers wanted to protect the people from the kind of lies and petty deceptions that have become standard practice in American politics today.

If this seems unbelievable, consider how prevalent the white lies of politicians are today, and how we've come to casually accept lying as a political necessity.

Consider how white lies become official deception once a candidate is elected to office.

Finally, consider that official deception was unheard of during the period of our history when candidates conducted modest front porch campaigns, did not seek the limelight, and spoke to the people through surrogates and *intermediaries*.

Today, candidates crisscross the country seeking applause from anyone who will listen, and much of what they have to say is either empty rhetoric or outright falsehood.

All of this suggests that perhaps the framers were on to something.

After all, the framers created intermediary powers not to *distance* the people from their political leaders, but to *protect* the people from the unruly ambition and potentially sinister designs of demagogues.

With the intent of the framers in mind, let's look at the concerted assault waged against intermediary powers during the so-called Progressive Era.

During the Progressive Era, the intermediary powers in our political system were unsparingly criticized as "corrupt" and "undemocratic."[6]

Intermediaries were said to be tools of "boss rule," and were criticized for causing decisions to be made in "smoke-filled rooms," out of sight from the people.

Legislatures and party conventions came under attack; and the Progressive campaign against these intermediary institutions was a four-pronged assault.

First, "direct democracy"—in the form of the initiative and referendum—was established to bypass legislatures.

Second, recall elections were established to allow the removal of elected officials during their term of office.

Third, the direct election of senators was established under the assumption that ordinary people would thereby gain a direct role in choosing U.S. Senators.

Lastly, the direct primary system was adopted with the *purported* intent of empowering the people to select candidates.

What few care to admit is that each of these innovations made our system more susceptible to moneyed influence and less responsive to the people.

Even though this is the reality, many refuse to see the truth about these "reforms" even today, because the *truth* is so at odds with conventionally-accepted *assumptions*.

In the fog of passions that prevailed during the Progressive Era, few made any reckoning of the true cost of removing intermediaries from our political process.

We know, for example, that the indirect election of senators was intended by the framers of the Constitution to give the states a "power of self-defense"[7] against federal encroachment, by means of the U.S. Senate's power to veto legislation, treaties, and appointments.

The direct election of senators, established by the Seventeenth Amendment, *inherently undermines* the federal structure of our constitutional system.

Practically speaking, the Seventeenth Amendment repealed the Tenth Amendment, because it left states without a way of defending "The powers…reserved to the States"[8] within our federal system.[9]

But the direct election of senators was *not* the Progressives' most effective reform.

In the movement to dissolve intermediary powers, centralize power at the federal level, overturn the balance of power, and subvert our republican institutions, the prize of "most effective reform" most assuredly goes to the direct primary.

The effect of direct primary elections was greater than the effect of the direct election of senators, in part because many states were using the direct primary to bypass state legislatures even before direct election of senators became the law of the land.[10]

In this way, the direct primary destroyed the intermediary power of the state legislatures to select U.S. Senators, well before the proposed Seventeenth Amendment was even considered by Congress.

* * *

Embraced by politicians of both parties, the direct primary became the means by which a silent and unseen coup was carried out under our Constitution.

CARL JARVIS

In the name of "democracy," the direct primary was supposed to end "boss rule."

Instead, the direct primary transformed elected officials into the moral equivalent of political bosses.

The direct primary was supposed to end "corruption."

Instead, the primary system took moneyed influence in our politics to a staggering new level.

The direct primary was supposed to end decision-making in "smoke-filled rooms." Instead, it moved the smoke-filled rooms to the lobbyists' offices and inner sanctums of power in Washington.

These consequences, though seemingly unintended, all sprang from the principal effect of the direct primary.

By destroying the intermediary power of party leaders and active citizens within the party system, the direct primary hollowed out the organizational structures previously found at the heart of our republican institutions.

The direct primary made party intermediaries into passive spectators without any real power to challenge elected officials, much to the detriment of our republican form of government.

The direct primary was so effective in eliminating intermediaries, that it would be hard to imagine a surer way to destroy government of, by, and for the people.

* * *

Since its adoption, the direct primary has overturned our republican institutions by engaging all the frailties of human nature on the side of destruction.

Today, our system is so devoid of intermediary powers—and thus power has become so concentrated—that the abuse of power is now commonplace.

The danger of this concentration of power is revealed by recent scandals: the Justice Department's seizure of Associate Press journalists' records, the Internal Revenue Service's targeting of grassroots political organizations, and the National Security Agency's unauthorized domestic spying programs.

The granddaddy of all these was Watergate, which is now a byword for the abuse of power that's become a routine occurrence in Washington today.

Watergate may *seem* like an isolated incident, the work of a power-obsessed president and his henchmen.

But Watergate can be more fruitfully understood as the by-product of an institutional crisis that's only grown worse in the decades since Nixon resigned in disgrace.

Watergate reveals not only the dynamics of the concentration of power, but also how the concentration of power was fostered by direct primary elections.

After Watergate, there were those who recognized the deep connection between the primary election system, the dissolution of intermediary powers, and the conditions that gave rise to Watergate.

But since we've not done anything to fix the problem, the problem has only grown worse.

My own awareness of the connection between presidential primaries, the concentration of power in the presidency, and the conditions that led to Watergate began when I read James Ceaser's *Presidential Selection* many years ago. Of the Watergate scandal, he observed:

> On the Republican side, the Watergate break-in and the other assortment of dirty tricks were also linked to certain features of the selection system. These acts were the work of a wholly personal organization dedicated to the election of a

particular man. A party-run organization, it was often argued, would never have allowed itself to go to these extremes, as it would have been more independent of the candidate and less willing to sacrifice the long-term reputation of the party for the success of the individual.[11]

It's worth unpacking this statement to take a closer look at the link between presidential *primaries* and the ongoing abuse of presidential *power*, of which Watergate was but one instance.

Of the conditions that led to Watergate, it's worth focusing on two in particular: first, the flow of funds that paid for the burglary and cover-up; and, second, the unquestioning loyalty of the White House staff to the arbitrary will of one man.

* * *

The money used to pay for the Watergate burglary was drawn from the Committee to Re-Elect the President (also known as CREEP). Because the account was the campaign account of the president, the president personally controlled it; that is, no one else had a veto over the use of funds.

Direct personal control of campaign funds by the candidates may be less than ideal, but it is a practical necessity under the direct primary system.

Candidates need to build their own campaign organization in order to win nomination. There is no way to fund a personal campaign organization except for the candidate to control the funds. Once the nomination is won, party resources can be brought into the race. Until the nomination is decided, however, candidates must rely on their own resources.

Whether candidates *should* control the money is beside the point. Candidates *must* control the money because the logic of the direct primary process forces them to do so.

This problem is one that no campaign finance reform can remedy, because history shows the problem to be embedded in the way the direct primary system works.

The direct primary not only makes personal control of funds by candidates *necessary*; in doing so, it also removes an important check from our political process.

By way of contrast, campaign funds controlled by party organizations are very unlikely to be used for the scandalous ends brought to light by Watergate.

But candidate control of funds is just one aspect of the direct primary's candidate-centered structure, which causes far more serious problems as well.

* * *

The candidate-centered campaign organization— independent of political party, unaccountable to party leaders, and controlled by the arbitrary will of the candidate—is the real story at the heart of Watergate.

The personal campaign organization, like the personal control of funds, is an outgrowth of the direct primary, because direct primary elections leave the candidates to their own devices as they pursue nomination.

After a candidate wins nomination, and then election, the same consultants who advised the candidate share in the spoils of victory. They often join the staff of the new elected official, just as party workers would have entered government employment in the old days.

The difference between the new-style *campaign* organization and the old-style *party* organization lies not only in the stability and duration of each organization, but also in the loyalty and independence of staff under each system.

"Loyalty to person" and "loyalty to principle" are ultimately dictated by career concerns; but the incentives are very different under each system.

The danger of the staffing system we have today, under the direct primary, is that the entire system—both during the campaign and afterward—has come to revolve around the personal and arbitrary will of the candidate.

The candidate's advisors are intensely and even unquestioningly loyal to the candidate.

This loyalty has consequences for the makeup of the White House staff in particular.

Beginning in the 1960s, hiring practices for the White House staff began to change,[12] due to the rise of candidate-centered campaign organizations which grew out of the presidential direct primary system.

This evolution can be plainly seen in the history of White House staffing practices.

Before the presidency of Franklin Roosevelt, there wasn't much of a White House staff to speak of. It was during the Roosevelt administration that the White House staff began to grow by leaps and bounds.

By the early 1950s, the White House directly employed hundreds of people.

But it was the *hiring practices*, and not the *size* of the staff, which became a factor in Watergate.

Up through the end of the Eisenhower administration, White House staffers were hired on a referral basis with recommendations from state and congressional party leaders.

White House hiring practices changed after 1960, as the Kennedy administration sought to hire "the best and the brightest,"[13] without consulting party leaders.

The change reflected an increasingly candidate-centered arrangement in the presidential nominating process, and a concurrent loss of power by party leaders.

The shift in the relative power of party leaders and candidates was due to the rising number of states making use of presidential *direct* primary elections.

The change to White House hiring practices may have *seemed* inconsequential when it was made.

By the end of the 1960s, however, the effect of the change was beginning to show.

During the Johnson administration, and again during the Nixon administration, the White House hiring practices begun by President Kennedy were formalized.

With this shift, the vetting and hiring of White House staff was entirely withdrawn from the parties, and became an internal function of the White House.

Although objective criteria were used to vet candidates in the application process, loyalty to the president became an unspoken requirement in the hiring decision.

It's important to note that these new hiring practices emerged not by direction of any president, but rather out of the logic of the presidential primary process itself.

The new practices filled a vacuum that developed as the influence of party leaders waned.

As the nominating process came to center around the person of the candidate, the White House staff similarly became deformed around the person of the president.

The White House staff became a kind of imperial bodyguard around the president.

The staffing practices that grew out of the presidential primary system fostered a dangerous concentration of power in the presidency—an arrangement that would soon be dubbed "The Imperial Presidency."[14]

During the Johnson and Nixon administrations, the White House finally eliminated the last remnants of party involvement in its hiring and staffing decisions.

With the president's inner ring of advisors closely vetted for personal loyalty to the president, the table was set for an epic abuse of power to take place.

Given the chaotic state of the Democratic nominating race in 1972, Nixon would have been reelected without the intelligence sought through the Watergate break in.

Election considerations aside, the idea to conduct the break-in seems to have originated in the paranoia and groupthink that afflicted the White House staff—a staff that shared Nixon's preoccupation with the pursuit of power for its own sake.

The candidate-centered nominating system—and the staffing practices fostered by that system—left no one in the president's inner ring to offer sound, independent, or candid counsel.

The White House staff became so insulated from the outside world that a siege mentality developed; and the staff began to view any public scrutiny as hostile.

This was the source of the White House's fixation with secrecy, its pursuit of "leaks," and its downward spiral into criminal acts carried out by "the plumbers."

Given the unquestioning loyalty of the White House staff, it's no wonder that three of Nixon's senior-most advisors were later prosecuted and convicted for the roles they played in Watergate.

* * *

The Watergate scandal is a case study in the perils of a direct primary system devoid of the moderating influence of party organization.

Prior to 1960, party leaders around the country still had a fair degree of influence in the presidential nominating process of each party.

In 1932, for example, when Franklin Roosevelt sought the Democratic presidential nomination for the first time, his campaign manager Jim Farley crisscrossed the country lining up delegates well in advance of the convention.[15]

Roosevelt would not have won the nomination so easily—and perhaps not at all—without this prior effort.

By 1960, however, the role of convention delegates in deciding presidential nominees was in decline. With the conventions declining in influence, party organizations and party leaders began to decline in influence as well.

After 1960, power in the selection process began to shift from party organizations to candidates.

Kennedy's strategy for winning nomination in 1960 reflected this shift in power. He divided his efforts between courting party leaders and appealing directly to primary voters, and he won.[16]

The effect of the loosened bond between president and party that resulted was not obvious at the time, but would become increasingly evident as presidential direct primaries became prevalent.

It's no coincidence that the 1972 election—the first in which a majority of national convention delegates were selected via direct primary[17]—also witnessed presidential power run amok at Watergate.

These two historic events were closely interconnected.

With over half the convention delegates chosen by direct primary, the deliberative role of the national party conventions was dead, along with the intermediary role of party organizations, party leaders, and active citizens.

* * *

Many people continue to view Watergate in partisan terms—or in terms of Nixon's personal frailties—but they miss the larger warning trumpeted by Watergate.

Watergate indicated the failure of checks and balances, far more than it indicated the failure of any single person or small group.

Watergate can be most accurately understood as the product of a concentration of power wrought by the presidential primary system in effect at that time.

Worse yet, Watergate is only the most dramatic scandal of a type that's become commonplace under the presidential direct primary system *that we still use*.

The critical lesson of Watergate is still relevant today, because the same concentration of power that produced Watergate is still in effect today.

The removal of intermediaries from the nominating process is really no different than the removal of checks and balances from the Constitution itself.

Based on the account presented in this chapter, you may be tempted to think that problems created by the direct primary begin and end in the White House staff.

But the concentration of power that grew out of the dissolution of intermediaries assumes many forms today.

The appointment of regulatory czars without vetting or confirmation by the Senate is another demonstration of the concentration of power that prevails today.

And the growth of presidential lawmaking by fiat is yet another example.

The point is that the real problem is larger than the issue of White House staffing practices; and the problem won't be fixed in a piecemeal way, but only by overhauling the distribution of political power.

Thus the problem won't be fixed until we restore the role of active citizens within the presidential nominating process—by restoring the intermediary role of parties.

* * *

Direct primaries were adopted on the premise that party conventions were a mere tool of the bosses who decided the fate of the people in smoke-filled rooms.

Today, however, candidates hold the power that political bosses once did; and, once elected, they hold the power of elected office as well.

This is the root of the concentration of power we see today.

Today, instead of political bosses, we have candidates who pursue power and seek reelection without scruple.

Instead of party conventions, we have empty rituals to rubber-stamp the plurality winner of the primaries.

The type of candidate that prevails today is moved by blind ambition and insatiable hunger for power.

To restore sanity to our politics, the key is for active citizens to have the ability to meaningfully participate in the selection of their leaders; and such participation is dangerously lacking from our present system.

People may *feel* like they influence the result when they vote in a primary. But most people don't even bother to vote.

Of those who do vote in primaries, they're inevitably influenced by media and by paid advertising.

In this way, moneyed influence—operating from the very centers of power—exercises control over our entire political system.

If you want to understand why we have such centralization and concentration of power today, simply follow the money.

Even more frustrating is that primaries are often decided based on issues the candidates have no sincere desire to deal with. Often, primary election appeals have little to do with the office being sought.

Given the harmful effects of the dissolution of intermediary powers, will we work to restore the proper role of active citizens in our nominating process?

Or will we proceed further down the road to serfdom?

The choice is up to us.

7

Self-Government and the Permanent Campaign

Today politicians engage in endless campaigning that begins long before they seek higher office, and that ends only after they leave public life.

The "permanent campaign" consumes so much of an elected official's time and energy that it shapes their view of the world in every way possible.

Today, few elected officials have the courage to make any decision without considering its impact on their fund-raising and reelection prospects.

The permanent campaign disqualifies humble and unassuming candidates, and allows bold and reckless office seekers to rise to the top.

The demands of the permanent campaign favor those who are motivated by blind ambition.

And the same candidates who violate the bounds of decency in pursuit of office are often found engaging in unethical or illegal conduct once elected.

The preoccupation with campaigning, reelection, and pursuit of higher office does not only destroy responsible governance and hinder sound policymaking.

As the permanent campaign becomes the primary business of elected officials, it is destroying the ability of the people to govern themselves.

* * *

When Sidney Blumenthal gave a name to the interrelated activities he dubbed the "permanent campaign" in the early 1980s, he observed of the permanent campaign that it "remakes government into an instrument designed to sustain an elected official's popularity."[1]

During the decades since Blumenthal first offered this observation, the campaign mentality has become even more pervasive.

The campaign mentality now informs practically every decision made, every position taken, and every policy announced with fanfare by our elected officials.

In *The Permanent Campaign and Its Future*, Norman Ornstein and Thomas Mann observe the degree to which the campaign mentality affects the workings of government today:

> Candidates for the presidency and Congress now are in a perpetual campaign mode. Political consultants and pollsters occupy prominent staff positions with public officials. Fund-raising trumps all competitors in the struggle for the attention and energy of politicians and aides... The line between campaigning and governing has all but disappeared, with campaigning increasingly dominant.[2]

All of this may still seem harmless until you consider just how far some elected officials have gone in order to remain in power.

With this in mind, here's a working definition of the permanent campaign that's worth considering: *it is how power-hungry politicians conduct themselves when they're willing to say and do anything to remain in power.*

* * *

Despite the saturation of our political life with campaigns and campaign-like activities, the origin of the permanent campaign is not widely understood.

On the surface, the permanent campaign seems to stem from candidates selfishly jockeying for advantage.

At a deeper level, however, the permanent campaign is a consequence of direct primary elections, because the direct primary offers first-mover advantages to the candidate first to declare, first to organize, and first to begin raising money (*not necessarily in that order*).

This dynamic can be seen on a large scale in the presidential primary process, but the dynamic can be observed in primary races for every other office as well.

The first-mover advantage is so powerful that it even influences states as to when to hold primary elections. The prevailing belief is that the earlier a state holds its primary, the more influence the state will have on the presidential nominating decision of both parties. States pursue their interests accordingly.

The advantage of an early primary is thought so great that a few states have incurred penalties to hold their primaries earlier than allowed by party rules.

Today, the first-mover dynamic in the presidential nominating process has reached a logical limit as candidates are fundraising constantly, declaring their candidacies years in advance, all while states strive to hold their primaries as early as possible.

Critics of the current presidential primary system have proposed reforms to curb the constant campaigning that's become commonplace.

With the idea of leveling the playing field between candidates *and* between states, each presidential cycle finds op-ed writers at work advocating a national primary or series of regional primaries.

But the adoption of a national or regional primary would only intensify the fundraising pressures that already bear on the candidates. These proposals, if adopted, would only force viable candidates to begin campaigning even earlier than they do today.

To reduce the carnival-like spectacle of the presidential nominating process, other critics of the present system would prohibit personal campaigning, fundraising, or both, prior to a certain date each election cycle. But it's hard to see how such measures could coexist with freedom of speech, never mind the difficulty of enforcing them. In any case, such measures would not stop incumbents from engaging in campaign-like activities, under the guise of performing their duties.

Sorting through the confusion evident in these proposals, it's important to note that candidates are merely responding to incentives which originate in the direct primary system itself: incentives which none of the proposed reforms would go so far as to address.

The simple truth is this: candidates who are serious about winning do what the system demands; and they are selected accordingly. Meanwhile, the system ruthlessly culls those who ignore its demands.

In other words, candidates do not shape the system: they are *shaped by* the system. The nominating system, in particular, shapes—almost in a deterministic way—the behavior and temperament of those whom it selects.

Looking at it in this light, the permanent campaign is an *institutional* problem, rooted in the *system itself* and not merely in the *behavior* of candidates.

If the permanent campaign is a product of the direct primary system—a system that gives candidates every incentive to pursue their interests, even to the detriment of the public good—then it's not inconceivable that the primary system would cause other problems as well.

Let's look briefly at two.

Presidential primary elections—with their candidate-centered focus—practically force candidates to build cult-like followings. In *The Cult of the Presidency*, Gene Healy observes of one recent candidate:

> On the campaign trail, Obama simultaneously promised to roll back executive power and to greatly expand the bounties that the president can provide. And, whether by accident or design, he's become the focal point of an enormous and unsettling cult of personality.[3]

On the campaign trail, the "cult of the presidency" gives rise to all manner of nonsense and pandering. Translated into policy, it fosters unreal expectations that the president can (or should) fix every ill of society.

This style of appeal is not unique to one party, to one candidate, or to one election season; rather, *the style of appeal results from the unmediated and plebiscitary nature of the presidential direct primary system.*

Let's look at another effect of the presidential direct primary system on our political discourse.

The nature of the direct primary all but requires candidates to be outspoken on a wide range of issues, including many issues unrelated to their duties of office.

The constant verbal outpour of candidates has altered relations between government and the people; and this has altered how our political process works.

As Jeffrey Tullis observes in *The Rhetorical Presidency*:

> Since the presidencies of Theodore Roosevelt and Woodrow Wilson, popular or mass rhetoric has become a principal tool of presidential governance. Presidents regularly 'go over the heads' of Congress to the people at large in support of legislation and other initiatives.[4]

According to Tullis, this change in the posture of presidents was marked by a change from written to oral communications, and also by a shift in the logic of presidential rhetoric.

As Tullis observes of the trend in presidential rhetoric:

> 44 percent of the twentieth-century [Inaugural Addresses and State of the Union Messages] mention the Constitution as against 87 percent of the nineteenth-century messages.[5]

Thus in the flood of verbosity that gushes from the modern presidency, references to the Constitution that once undergirded presidential rhetoric have disappeared.

If presidents behave differently under the direct primary than they did before, it's because the party convention system was arranged around an entirely different set of incentives.

Not only did party conventions *fail to reward* the kind of behavior that it takes to win today; the conventions actually *punished* the antics that have become so typical under the direct primary system.

Alexis de Tocqueville saw the effects of campaigning on governance just as mass campaigning was getting underway in America, and he had this to say:

> The President, for his part, is absorbed in the task of defending himself. He no longer rules in the interest of the state, but in that of his own reelection; he prostrates himself before the majority, and often, instead of resisting their passions as duty requires, he hastens to anticipate their caprices.[6]

If Tocqueville's observation was true then, it's even more true now, as the permanent campaign now pervades our political process.

Today, the endless election cycle offers advantage to any candidate willing to seize the initiative, even those willing to ignore the common good in pursuit of power.

Meanwhile, the direct primary practically disqualifies any candidate who harbors *even a hint* of modesty about the grand designs they'll undertake once in office.

The direct primary favors candidates who are spurred by boundless ambition, and who have no scruple about trampling civil liberties and rule of law.

Candidates will *promise* anything to win election, but there's one thing they will not *do* once elected.

They will not leave you free to govern your affairs through local self-government; and their endless meddling *seems to stem* from the demands of an *unmediated* nominating process.

Under the direct primary, candidates must be all things to all people; the system is *inherently hostile* to leaving the people free to control their own lives.

Under the direct primary, candidates ply a kind of ruthless manipulation to win nomination; and their desire for control only grows once they're elected.

This isn't to say that good people don't get elected here and there. But the exceptions are too few in number to make a real difference.

In every important respect, the permanent campaign and its effects are true and faithful offspring of the direct primary system.

The permanent campaign is a danger to the country, a threat to the people, and a menace to what remains of self-government in America.

But we cannot fix the *problem* unless we fix the *system*.

PART III

Ground Zero:
The Destruction of
Republican Institutions
1910-1925

Today American politics is beset by polarization, dysfunction, and abuse of power.

The chaotic condition of our political process is slowly submerging civil liberty and rule of law.

These problems may *seem* unrelated, but they're really all symptoms of the same root cause.

To see the true nature of the crisis we face, we need to take a long-term view; and we need to carefully examine the institutional nature of the crisis.

If so many of our problems *seem* intractable today, then it's worth looking deeper at the structural changes that created those problems in the first place.

Direct primaries affect more than the tenure of incumbents, the distribution of political power, and the conduct of political campaigns.

Direct primaries also affect the procedures, forms, and structures of virtually every other institution we use to govern ourselves.

To see the wide ranging effects of direct primaries on our political system, it's important to begin with a few preliminary observations.

First, the history of the nominating process—like the broader history of our political institutions—can be divided into three periods.

The first period originated with the establishment of our Constitution; the second period began in the 1830s and ended in the 1910s; and the third period is where we find ourselves today.

Of the three major nominating systems we've used— the congressional caucus, the party convention system, and the direct primary—the party convention system was a moderate choice between extremes.

In contrast, the direct primary—both in its nature and in its effect on our political system—is the most *extreme* system we're ever used.

It follows as a natural consequence that *the direct primary has pushed every other facet of our political institutions to an extreme* as well.

This fact is obvious when our political system is viewed on a long historical timeline, from the formation of our Constitution to the present day.

Look at the history of our political institutions—from the committee organization of Congress to the structure of the federal judiciary—and it's clear that we're at an extreme in *every major facet* of the institutions we use to govern ourselves.

These extreme institutional arrangements lie at the *root* of the crippling dysfunction that paralyzes our system today.

Thus, if we're to restore our capacity for self-government, we must begin by recalling the history of the institutions we've used to govern ourselves.

Only then will we have the chance to unravel those long-forgotten "reforms" that lie at the root of the crisis we face today.

8

The Beginning of a Congressional Revolution

Today Congress's approval rating stands at an all-time low. And it's no wonder why: Congress, as an institution, no longer serves to represent the people.

Instead, Congress has abdicated its spending and lawmaking powers to executive agencies and lobbyists.

There's no shortage of proposals offered to correct this state of affairs; and many of the most popular proposals would involve amending the Constitution.

To reign in deficit spending, for example, we're told that we need an amendment to balance the budget.

To end Congress's delegation of lawmaking power to the executive, we're told that we need an amendment to restore the separation of powers.

Never mind that these amendment proposals would be extremely difficult to pass.

Never mind that they would not materially alter the conduct or workings of Congress as an institution.

Never mind that they would be no more likely to be enforced by the courts than the rest of the Constitution.

The larger question concerning Congress's abdication of power is often overlooked: somehow, Congress performed well, for over a century, before becoming incapacitated and incapable of performing its duties.

Since no constitutional amendment *caused* the problem in the first place, it logically follows that no constitutional amendment will *fix* the problem.

In fact, a careful look at history suggests that the problem has nothing to do with the Constitution.

The reason Congress no longer does its job is because of changes that began unfolding *inside* Congress over a century ago.

* * *

If changes inside Congress made Congress unable to function properly, those changes can be traced to a relatively unknown incident that occurred in 1910.

This event is often referred to as the Congressional Revolution of 1910; and it's no exaggeration to call it a revolution.

Examine the history of Congress and you'll discover that the last century of congressional reorganization and dysfunction began with this little-known incident.

The Congressional Revolution of 1910 is not only an important event in the history of Congress; it's also an important event in the history of our Constitution.

Our Constitution is supposed to secure a republican form of government, which assumes an independent legislature and a balance of power between the branches.

But the change in 1910 undermined the power of Congress, even to the extent of making the balance of power impossible to preserve.

The Constitution made Congress the "first branch," but the Congressional Revolution made Congress into a second-rate ward of the executive branch.

On the surface, the Congressional Revolution of 1910 was a revolt against the personal rule of then-Speaker of the House Joseph G. Cannon.

The "revolt" against Cannon was carried out by a simple majority vote that changed the rules of the House and altered the powers of the Speaker of the House.

The vote *seemed* to be a protest against the will of one man who happened to be serving as Speaker.

But the vote would have consequences far beyond Cannon's tenure in office.

The simple majority vote initiated a dramatic change to the distribution of power inside Congress.

Soon, the change in the distribution of power began to adversely affect the internal workings of Congress.

Although the vote was nominally a vote against one man, it was symbolically a vote against the precedents and traditions of the House which had long served as a bulwark of our republican institutions.

And although the vote is scarcely remembered a century later, its effect in weakening the Speaker of the House was immediate; and it still hobbles Congress today.

The basic settlement forged by the Congressional Revolution persists in part because many accounts of the history of Congress have failed to observe the wide-ranging effects of that simple majority vote.

* * *

Prior to the Congressional Revolution, the Speaker of the House held three important parliamentary powers.

First, the Speaker appointed all members of all committees, including the chairmen. This allowed the Speaker to make the best use of each member's expertise.

Second, the Speaker chaired and appointed all members of the Rules Committee. This gave the Speaker control of the flow of business on the House floor.

Third, the Speaker referred all bills to committees. This allowed the Speaker to manage workloads and coordinate lawmaking throughout Congress.

The Speaker exercised these powers by consent of the majority, and the powers were held in check by the Speaker's election at the beginning of each new term.

In theory, the House majority could vote "no confidence" at any time, and force the Speaker to resign.

The "no confidence" vote would be an innovation to our system, but such a practice would have done far less damage than the Congressional Revolution of 1910.

* * *

Even before the storm clouds of revolt appeared on the horizon, Speaker of the House Joe Cannon was pitted against powerful forces.

Democrats in Congress opposed Cannon's policies and did what they could to obstruct his efforts.

Cannon also faced opposition within his own party, from the so-called Insurgent Republicans. We'll examine the Insurgents' role in the Congressional Revolution in just a moment.

Cannon also had to contend with senior members of Congress who had long served as committee chairmen, and who were increasingly jealous of Cannon's power.

This conflict between the Speaker and the committee chairmen was especially contentious; and it was only a matter of time before it would explode into a struggle.

Lastly, Cannon was up against the effects of the newly-established direct primary system.

Direct primaries were unleashing the kind of populist, personality-driven politics we take for granted today; and the Insurgent Republicans typified the new style.

The Insurgents bristled at party discipline, rejected consensus, and reveled in obstructionism.

It's no coincidence that the Insurgents were mostly nominated by direct primary, a device used in relatively few states prior to the election of 1908.[1]

* * *

The Insurgent Republicans began their public attack against Cannon in the 1908 House elections.

Although the Republican Party won a majority in the House, the Insurgent Republicans held the balance of power between the Republican majority and the Democratic minority.

The Insurgents challenged Cannon's reelection as Speaker, but lacked the votes to choose someone else.

Opposition to Cannon continued to build throughout the term.

Then, on March 16, 1910, the epic showdown that would become known as the Congressional Revolution of 1910 began.

For months, George Norris—a Republican from Nebraska and leader of the Insurgents—had been carrying in his pocket a resolution designed to strip parliamentary power from the Speaker of the House.

During the debate of a census bill, Norris saw his opportunity and pounced.

The resolution Norris presented would have removed the Speaker from the Rules Committee, tripled the size of the Rules Committee, and taken away the Speaker's power to appoint members of all standing committees.

The resolution became the subject of a 26-hour debate.

Cannon's supporters rallied to his defense—and to the defense of Congress—but it wasn't enough.

After Norris amended his resolution to allow the Speaker to retain the power to appoint House committee members, the resolution passed.

The vote taken that day had sweeping implications for our form of government.

Yet at the moment it was taken, the vote was really a "no confidence" vote against Cannon himself.

It's ironic, then, that when Cannon offered to resign shortly after the vote, his resignation was not accepted.

The refusal of the majority to remove Cannon from the speakership indicates the recklessness of their entire plan of action.

The revolt against Cannon typified the kind of mob mentality that seeks to destroy without offering a better alternative. This mentality permeates Congress today.

The refusal to remove Cannon—a man whom they denounced as "czar" and "tyrant"—also testifies to a profound lack of clarity in their aims.

They seem to have confused the speakership and its power with the man who happened to occupy the office at the time.

Viewing the entire episode from a distance, it would *seem* the Insurgents could have satisfied their aim simply by removing Cannon from the office *while leaving the powers of the office intact.*

Instead they destroyed the powers of the office—and along with it, the power of Congress—while allowing Cannon to remain in office for the balance of the term.

Cannon was removed from the Rules Committee and the size of the committee was tripled, per the resolution.

But Cannon retained his influence over the committee through surrogates that he appointed.

Thus in the immediate aftermath of the historic vote, not much *seemed* to have changed.

As a result of the election later that year, a Democratic majority took control of the House; and then the effects of the Congressional Revolution began to take hold.

The new majority confirmed the rules established by the Norris resolution, but also went further.

The House majority that passed the Norris revolution had been unwilling to strip the Speaker of the power to appoint House committee members.

But the new House majority had no such reservation.

Prospective Speaker Champ Clark went along with the rule change because he could not have cared less. He was already planning to run for the presidency; he viewed his tenure as Speaker as a stepping stone.

Champ Clark not only had no interest in resisting the change on grounds of principle, but also no interest in defending the prerogatives of Congress as an institution.

* * *

The change brought about by the Congressional Revolution of 1910 was, without a doubt, constitutional in its significance.

The change was constitutional in significance because it completely altered the distribution of power between Congress and the presidency.

But the constitutional significance of the change is often overlooked; after all, the Speaker was vested with the power to appoint committees by decision of the House and not by the Constitution.

Because the Constitution leaves such matters to "Each House,"[2] people tend to overlook the constitutional impact of congressional rules and organization.

The power to appoint House committees was vested in the speakership beginning in 1790. The office retained the appointment power continuously until 1911.[3]

The growth of the House—from 106 members in 1790 to 435 in 1911—only made the Speaker's power to appoint committees that much more important.

By Cannon's day, the Speaker's appointment power was not just a matter of tradition.

It was arguably the glue that held the House together, without which the House would have flown apart—*like it did after 1910*—in 435 different directions.

The Speaker's power to appoint committees was the lynchpin that preserved a workable distribution of power within the House; in so doing, the Speaker's power worked to preserve the balance of power between Congress and the presidency.

In other words, the separation of powers provided by the Constitution had come to depend on a parliamentary power nowhere mentioned in the Constitution.

The House majority had tacitly acknowledged the importance of the Speaker's appointment power when it declined to eliminate that power in 1910.

But the new House majority of 1911 apparently either did not see—or did not care—that its removal of the Speaker's appointment power would fatally weaken Congress within the broader political system.

* * *

A decade after the Congressional Revolution had run its course, *Washington Post* columnist George Brown remarked at the "system of secret government"[4] that had taken root within Congress.

Speaker Joe Cannon had been a lightning rod for criticism because everyone knew where he stood.

People knew Cannon was responsible, in large part, for the policies enacted or rejected by Congress.

But as the speakership's power was transferred to faceless entities like party caucuses, *leadership* of the House—along with *responsibility* for the actions of the House—began to vanish into thin air.

As the party caucuses began exercising the power to appoint House committees, the criteria used to make committee assignments changed.

No longer were committee assignments made according to the policy objectives of the majority. Appointments were now based on the preferences of senior members of the House.

The shift benefitted the longest-serving members of the House who were serving as committee chairman or who were in line to become committee chairs.

The new "seniority system" brought about a dramatic redistribution of power within the House; and the redistribution naturally favored the chairmen.

It was not long before the chairmen began to flex their newly-won power and independence.

The first aftershock of the Congressional Revolution was felt soon afterward when the committee chairmen consolidated their power by reducing the number of standing committees.

This first consolidation, like others that would follow, was supposedly done to increase the efficiency of Congress; and it affected only a few committees.

But looking at this first consolidation in light of all others that followed, it's worth noting that the number of standing committees in the House reached an all-time peak around this time.

The standing committees have not since approached—much less exceeded—the number that existed in 1910.

Committee consolidation had two major effects.

First, it gave the committees that remained—and their chairmen—larger jurisdiction. This gave the committee chairmen more power.

Second, it yielded a committee organization in the House that was less specialized than before.

This meant the committee chairmen and members would bring less expertise to bear in drafting legislation.

The reorganization of the committee system impaired the legislative capacity of Congress, and led to an observable decline in the *quality* of lawmaking.

Within the space of a decade, Congress was reduced to rubber-stamping bills introduced by the president.

Of the bills Congress wrote, many simply delegated vast, unchecked rulemaking power to executive agencies.

During the decade after 1910, laws granting delegated rulemaking power to executive and administrative agencies *exceeded the number and scope of all such delegations* made in the history of Congress *prior to 1910.*

The explosive growth of delegated lawmaking was a *direct consequence* of the reorganization of Congress brought about by the Congressional Revolution of 1910.

* * *

The next aftershock of the Congressional Revolution rattled as committee chairmen moved to consolidate their control over the power of the purse.

Prior to the Civil War, powers to tax and spend were vested in a single House Ways and Means Committee.

In 1865, the spending power was given its own House Appropriations Committee.

And by the early twentieth century, the spending power was distributed among *twenty* committees, each with the power to authorize spending in specific areas.

Despite the wide dispersion of the spending power, Congress continued to pass balanced budgets because the Speaker still had the power to veto spending.

Increasingly, it fell to the Speaker to reconcile expenditures against revenue.

But the committee chairmen's desire for power would soon cause Congress to lose control of the purse strings.

After the Congressional Revolution, the Speaker became increasingly unable to prioritize demands within the budgetary process.

During the decade after 1910, Congress was running a cumulative budget deficit for the decade—even before the World War I build up—which exceeded most prior peacetime deficits spanning a similar multiyear period.[5]

In other words, with the decline of the speakership, Congress became inclined toward deficit spending to a degree *far greater than it had been prior to 1910.*

After a decade of budgetary chaos, including the uncontrolled deficits of World War I, Congress agreed to transfer a portion of its spending power to the president.

Congress surrendered its spending power through the Budget and Accounting Act of 1921.

The Budget Act was the first of a long line of reforms in which Congress abdicated its power to the executive in an effort to curb uncontrolled deficit spending.

Reforms like the Budget Act have done little to curb deficits over the long run; and deficit spending actually *increased* after many of the major reforms became law.

Reforms like the Budget Act have mainly served to aggrandize executive power while diminishing Congress' power of the purse.

Today, the executive branch either writes its own budget or is given automatic spending authorization through continuing resolutions.

Despite promises to the contrary, executive-led budget procedures have only led to *increased* deficit spending.

* * *

Although Congress has undergone many reforms since the Congressional Revolution, the reforms have all shared a common, fatal flaw.

None of the reforms since 1910 have reversed the damage done by that series of innovations that dismantled the office of the speakership.

Today we watch in dismay as the dysfunction of Congress imperils our republican form of government.

Yet we can't hope to fix the problem until the real issue is clearly defined.

The Congressional Revolution began as a populist insurgency against the Speaker of the House.

The insurgency resulted in a mob-like dismantlement of important, time-tested traditions within Congress.

Today, many people find the incompetence of Congress unacceptable, because it's left the executive in control of lawmaking and spending.

Yet many people would also refuse to *strengthen* the leadership of Congress, which is what is needed to actually solve the problem.

But even this ignores the larger issue.

It's hard to imagine widespread acceptance of a stronger Speaker of the House unless rotation in office were first restored in the House of Representatives.

It's also hard to imagine members of Congress adopting a reform that would curb their power, unless the members themselves underwent rotation in office.

Lastly, it's hard to imagine members of Congress agreeing to any sensible action, given the fog of faux populism that enshrouds the Capitol today.

This is all to say that abolition of the direct primary will probably have to come first, before any sensible changes can be made *within* Congress.

This line of thinking gives rise to a provocative question: would we strengthen Congress, even if it meant that some would *call* the Speaker of the House a *dictator*?

Or would we rather have a *weak* Congress, along with an unchecked dictator in the *presidency*?

The choice is ours.

9

The Rebirth of the
Rotten Boroughs

Today many people are at a loss to understand the controversy surrounding voter ID laws.

Opponents of voter ID claim that any requirement to show photo identification *suppresses* your right to vote.

Advocates of voter ID say that your right to vote is being destroyed by voter *fraud*.

But the real story of what's happening is being lost in all the sound and fury.

The voter ID controversy distracts from the *systematic* destruction of your right to vote via redistricting; and the voter ID issue seems *tailor made* to prevent this larger issue of gerrymandering from being dealt with.

If voter suppression and voter fraud present "retail" threats to the integrity of elections, then gerrymandering is the "wholesale" destruction of your right to vote.

The same politicians who make voter ID an issue are strangely silent while they conspire to steal your right to vote through gerrymandering.

Despite the heated controversy around voter ID, lawmakers find a ready *bipartisan* consensus when it comes to redrawing their own district lines.

In many cases, "bipartisan" redistricting plans *guarantee* the reelection of incumbents even while voters grow more disgusted with the incumbent political class.

Gerrymandering—and incumbency gerrymandering, in particular—is worse than ever today.

The effects of incumbency gerrymandering dwarf the ballot security issues which gave rise to the voter ID laws.

The problem is so bad that it's not only undermining elections and destroying public confidence in the system.

Extreme incumbency gerrymandering is destroying the very fabric of our republican institutions.

* * *

The reality of redistricting is so obscured today, in a maze of court rulings, that few understand the process well enough to see the forest from the trees.

Those who do understand the requirements tend to be the very same political insiders who routinely turn redistricting to their own benefit.[1]

Remarkably—despite high-level scrutiny by the federal courts—the abuse of the redistricting power has not only continued; it has actually grown worse since the courts began intervening in redistricting in the early 1960s.

The problem is that the courts refuse to recognize the full scope of practices that constitute gerrymandering.[2]

Simply put, gerrymandering is the manipulation of election district boundaries to guarantee—or to render more probable—a predetermined election outcome.

But the federal courts, in their exceeding wisdom, have given gerrymandering a much narrower definition.

Consequently, the major political parties are able to invoke the color of law and judicial precedent to justify their shameless gerrymandering schemes.

Gerrymandering was once a tool used exclusively by the majority party to maximize its election prospects.

Today, gerrymandering is far more often used to ensure the reelection of incumbents, regardless of party.

This is one reason why 80% of members of the House are routinely elected by margins of 60% or more today.[3]

Far from demonstrating the popularity of incumbents, the results demonstrate that most elections today are determined in advance by gerrymandering.

* * *

To understand how the courts provide cover to gerrymandering today, it helps to take a look at the entire history of redistricting in the United States.

Many people believe that gerrymandering began with the 1812 redistricting of Massachusetts, which was the incident that led to the coinage of the word.

As historian Elmer Griffith observed of the 1812 gerrymander, "the twenty-nine Democratic senators [afterward elected] were elected by a smaller vote than the eleven Federalist senators received."[4]

So it's certainly true that this was a skillful instance of the gerrymander.

But as Griffith went on to observe, the "skill displayed in manipulating the districts…was the best proof that the practice had antedated that time."[5]

In assessing the origins of the gerrymander, Griffith speculated that the practice was "as old as…popular election by districts,"[6] a time that would long predate the 1812 gerrymander.

We know also that the "rotten boroughs" were discussed at the Federal Convention.[7] Old Sarum, the most famous of the English rotten boroughs, was even mentioned by name.[8]

Old Sarum continued to elect two members to the British Parliament into the 1830s, when only a handful of absentee landowners made up its entire voter roll.

Although the framers discussed the issue, they did not move to curb the practice of gerrymandering in any way.

The silence of the Constitution on the redistricting issue makes the Supreme Court's extreme intervention in redistricting—*under the guise of interpreting the Constitution*—all the more incomprehensible.

* * *

The 1812 gerrymander provoked public outrage in part because it was so effective, but also because the manipulation was so blatant when viewed on a map.

Today, at a time when bizarrely drawn districts are commonplace, many have come to associate gerrymandering with visual offensiveness.

Historically, however, subtler and less visible practices were the norm.

Historically, the dominant form of gerrymandering was to draw districts grossly unequal in population, in order to favor one party at the expense of the other.

Districts were also drawn with separate sections containing disjoined land areas;[9] and with distorted boundary lines[10] that disregarded existing political subdivisions.

In many cases, redistricting was carried out at the whim of the majority, rather than immediately after the census.

Lastly, multi-member legislative districts were sometimes used instead of single-member districts, to completely prevent the election of the minority party.

Historically, *all six* of these practices were used—sometimes even in the same plan—while any *one* would constitute gerrymandering in a broad sense of the term.

Today, federal law and judicial precedent prohibit only two of these practices: unequal districts and multi-member districts.

This leaves lawmakers tremendous latitude to exploit redistricting to their own self-seeking advantage.

* * *

Alongside the rogue's gallery of gerrymandering practices, any account of the history of redistricting would be incomplete without mentioning the attempts to curb these practices.

Prior to 1910, there was a steady movement within Congress to regulate congressional redistricting under federal law.

Redistricting regulations were brought into effect through the acts of Congress that reapportioned representatives among the states, after each census.

In 1842, for example, Congress enacted a requirement for members of the House to be elected from contiguous, single-member districts. This meant districts had to be internally connected throughout and not separated by the land of an intervening district.[11]

In 1872, Congress required its districts to contain "as nearly as practicable an equal number of inhabitants."[12]

In 1901, Congress required its districts to be compact, which meant each point of a district's boundary was to be as close to the center of the district as possible. This was to prevent the kind of grossly distorted boundaries that are commonplace today.

The gradual movement to regulate congressional redistricting under federal law *seemed* to have reached completeness in 1901, when *all three* redistricting requirements were enacted all at once, for the first time.[13]

Congress again included *all three* redistricting requirements in the Apportionment Act of 1911,[14] before mysteriously abandoning any and all effort to regulate congressional redistricting under federal law.

The breakdown of redistricting regulations after 1911 demands attention for many reasons, not least because the trend corresponds to other changes that were afoot.

We saw in the last chapter that Congress began relinquishing its power to the executive around this time.

And it wasn't long before Congress would give up its redistricting power as well.

For over a century, Congress consistently passed a new apportionment law after each decennial census.

But after the 1920 census, Congress's consistency was interrupted. It took Congress nearly a decade to pass a new apportionment act.

This naturally affected representation, as some states retained representatives in Congress that should have been elected from other states.

The deadlock of the 1920s affected redistricting as well, because state legislatures had no reason to redraw congressional districts while the standoff persisted.

And the standoff affected redistricting in still another way: by the time the new apportionment bill became law, Congress had omitted from it all prior redistricting requirements.

Thus when the Apportionment Act of 1929 *finally* passed—nearly a decade overdue—it did not incorporate any of the redistricting requirements Congress had previously enacted over a period of seventy years.[15]

* * *

The 1920s reapportionment dispute is often explained in terms of urban-rural conflict,[16] but this explanation leaves much to be desired.

While it is true that rural areas of the country stood to lose representation due to the migration of Americans into cities, this was *not* a new issue in the 1920s.

This was an issue in *every reapportionment ever carried out* in the history of the country.

Thus it would seem that the decade-long stalemate was really just another episode in an increasingly consistent pattern of political dysfunction.

And the same dysfunction that delayed the Act also resulted in the omission of ·the redistricting requirements.

Although it may appear otherwise, congressional dysfunction is not actually due to *specific* political issues.

Rather, congressional dysfunction is largely the result of the *general* polarization caused by the direct primary.

It's also not a coincidence that the stalemate of the 1920s—for every year while it lasted—very much served the interests of incumbents. Some members of Congress would have seen their districts eliminated; and others would have seen their districts redrawn.

This is not to say the standoff was a *deliberate* effort by incumbents to remain in office. That would be attributing more sense than is warranted.

It's only to observe that the direct primary system may entrench incumbents in ways beyond its immediate effects.

* * *

The omission of redistricting requirements from the Apportionment Act of 1929 would have long-lasting consequences—consequences that are still felt today.

In 1932, the Supreme Court held that Congress's omission of redistricting requirements meant the requirements were no longer in force under federal law.[17]

The ruling was more a refusal by the Court to weigh in than a decision on the merits of the case.

The 1932 ruling nonetheless aided and abetted the kind of no-holds-barred gerrymandering that was taking over the redistricting process.

In 1946, the Supreme Court again refused to weigh in on the redistricting question. This time, in *Colegrove v. Green*, the Court spoke of the imprudence of allowing the courts to enter the "political thicket" and "involve the judiciary in the politics of the people."[18]

But the issue in *Colegrove* was different than in the earlier case: the *Colegrove* case arose not because of gerrymandering per se, but because of the Illinois state legislature's refusal to reapportion or redistrict the state's congressional seats *at any point after 1901.*

The situation in *Colegrove* was eerily reminiscent—in its facts and in its timing—to what occurred in Congress during the 1920s; even the supposed explanation, in terms of urban-rural conflict, was eerily similar.

In all likelihood, the breakdown in Illinois occurred for the same reason as the stalemate in Congress during the 1920s. In both cases, the Supreme Court washed its hands of the problem and declined to intervene.[19]

* * *

If state legislatures' refusal to redistrict was a problem in the 1940s, as evidenced by *Colegrove*, the problem became a crisis in the decades that followed.

By the early 1960s, for example, legislative districts in Tennessee hadn't been redrawn since 1901. During the intervening decades, the state's inhabitants had moved from rural to urban areas and from the western to the eastern part of the state.[20]

The problem had become so bad that just 40% of Tennessee's inhabitants were electing two-thirds of the members of the Tennessee House of Representatives.[21]

Representation in the state senate was even more skewed; and the problem affected congressional districts as well.

The situation was so bad that it gave rise to claims of "taxation without representation," since most taxes were being paid by districts that were heavily underrepresented in the legislature.[22]

The leaders who ran the legislature had no incentive to redistrict since they came from the same rural districts that stood to lose power under any conceivable redistricting plan.

This condition was not unique to Tennessee, but prevailed also in Florida, Minnesota, Oklahoma, Illinois, and in many other states.[23]

By the early 1960s, the situation was so bad—not only in Tennessee but around the country—that it gave rise to the famous Supreme Court case *Baker v. Carr*.[24]

As *Baker v. Carr* worked its way through the courts, many people had serious doubts about the power of *any* court to resolve the political issue of redistricting. There were also those who simply did not believe the courts should intervene in the redistricting process.

Given these concerns, it's not surprising that the *Baker v. Carr* ruling did not offer a remedy, so delicate was the Court's position in accepting the case in the first place.[25]

Rather than providing a remedy, the Supreme Court instead merely asserted jurisdiction over the question, and returned the case to the federal district court that originally heard it.

Although many problematic rulings followed in the wake of *Baker v. Carr*, singling out the *Baker* ruling as "government by judiciary"[26] rather misses the point.

The same lawmakers who stood to lose power under any conceivable redistricting plan were holding the system hostage in their longstanding refusal to redistrict.

Although *Baker v. Carr* is heavily criticized, it's hard to imagine how such a widespread redistricting crisis could have been resolved through the political process.

* * *

The trouble with *Baker v. Carr* began just a few years later, when the Supreme Court began applying the ruling indiscriminately, in ways that seemed to venture far beyond the modest scope of the original ruling.

Within two years of *Baker v. Carr*, the Court had announced its "one person, one vote"[27] doctrine, which is the Court's requirement that all single-member legislative districts contain roughly equal population.

The case in question, known as *Gray v. Sanders*, involved districts used for gubernatorial elections in Georgia.

That this case had nothing to do with legislative representation per se was an ominous sign of things to come.

Soon, the Court was applying its "one person, one vote" doctrine to congressional districts, state senate districts, and even local election districts.[28]

Not only was the Court beginning to invade the rightful domain of the state legislatures. The Court was also applying its "one person, one vote" doctrine to situations where the plain intent had been to provide a method of apportionment *other than* population.[29]

In one case, the Court even struck down a legislative reapportionment plan recently approved by Colorado voters.[30] In another, the Court struck down a Missouri redistricting plan that involved a 6% population difference between the largest and smallest district.[31] In yet another case, the Court struck down a New Jersey plan that called for a 0.7% population variation.[32]

In this manner, the Court bludgeoned states with its "one person, one vote" doctrine to the point of absurdity.

Even worse, in wielding its "one person, one vote" doctrine, the Court was *ignoring* partisan redistricting.[33] The Court was also ignoring redistricting requirements like "compactness" and "integrity of county lines."[34]

Thus through its *extreme judicial activism*, the Court was *passively* allowing the intensity of gerrymandering to skyrocket.

From a modest, necessary, and even praiseworthy effort to *protect* the right to vote, the rulings that followed in the aftermath of *Baker v. Carr* began to systematically *undermine* the right to vote.

* * *

Since *Baker v. Carr*, the Court has upheld redistricting plans that plainly favor incumbents,[35] as well as plans that plainly favor one party at the expense of the other.[36]

Given the Court's very narrow interpretation of its own doctrine, lawmakers have been given an unlimited license to violate the *spirit* of the "one person, one vote" doctrine with impunity.

These developments have now gone so far that it's fair to ask whether we've lost more of our voting rights than we've gained, due to the Supreme Court's continuous meddling in the "political thicket" of redistricting.

The Supreme Court's record is so bad that it's fair to ask whether our present redistricting crisis can be alleviated, so long as the courts remain so deeply insinuated in the redistricting process.

Because the courts now do so much to promote extreme incumbency gerrymandering, it's worth recalling why the courts got so involved in the first place.

Why was it, after all, that Illinois, Tennessee, and many other states, all stopped redistricting after 1901, for a period of *sixty years*?

Why was it that Congress became so unwilling—or unable—to include redistricting standards in the 1929 reapportionment, after including such standards for a period of *seventy years*?

Why was it that the entire reapportionment and redistricting process suddenly came undone *between 1901 and 1929*, after working smoothly for over a century?

The problem at the heart of these questions is far bigger than the mere problem of gerrymandering.

The problem encompasses political polarization and congressional dysfunction, and the problem reaches to the very heart of our capacity to govern ourselves.

Is it really a coincidence that Tennessee and other states were ahead of Congress by a decade, in showing the outward signs of dysfunction, given that Tennessee and other states adopted the direct primary a decade earlier than the rest of the country?

Is it really a coincidence that the problems in Tennessee and Illinois began after the 1910 census—and *not after* the 1920 census *or after* the 1900 census?

Furthermore, why was it that Congress's problems were delayed by a decade, comparatively speaking, so that they emerged only after the 1920 census?

The pattern in Tennessee, Illinois, and in the nation at large, seems clear.

The historical record *seems* to show that there is a direct link between the adoption of the direct primary, the rise of entrenched incumbency, and the interruption of redistricting in many states.

If this pattern holds—and if it's more than just a striking coincidence—it would reveal a set of issues that deeply affect public confidence in our political system.

There is little doubt that extreme gerrymandering—like entrenched incumbency—is destroying people's faith in our system of self-government.

While some look to the courts to fix the problem, the courts' efforts to deal with gerrymandering have been counterproductive to say the least.[37]

In any event, gerrymandering is—and will remain—very much a *political* problem.

Gerrymandering stems from the power of lawmakers to redistrict on their own behalf, *without having to answer to anyone but themselves.*

Thus the *extreme* gerrymandering we see today is really an outgrowth of the elimination of checks and balances from our system of nomination and election.

In this sense, incumbency gerrymandering results just as much from the dissolution of intermediary powers, as from the failure of redistricting regulations per se.

Viewing the problem in this light, it seems unlikely that we will curb the abuse of the redistricting process unless we first eliminate the direct primary.

By restoring intermediary powers, we'll not only curb the worst excesses of incumbency gerrymandering; we'll revitalize our entire system of self-government as well.

10

The Development of a Matrix of Dictatorship

Never before in the history of our country have people felt more threatened by out-of-control government; and never before was the threat more real than it is today.

As private sector workers watch their wages and job security diminish, their public sector counterparts enjoy rising wages and permanent employment.

The same public employees who enjoy permanent job security are also responsible for issuing tens of thousands of new regulations every year that make private sector jobs *less secure*.

On top of it all, public employees have the authority to enforce their arbitrary edicts at the point of a gun.

While all this is happening, government spending increases at an alarming rate and even modest proposals to cut spending provoke alarm.

Given this state of affairs, it seems fair to ask what's become of our country.

Politicians pay lip service to limited government—and to reducing the *size* of government—but they never seem to get around to actually doing anything about it.

The real problem is seldom mentioned: government workers are overpaid—and thus have little reason to leave the public sector—and they can't be fired.

These incentives have fostered a bureaucracy insulated from the people it purports to serve.

And this draws a fair question: are not these public *servants* increasingly the *masters* of our commonwealth?

* * *

The hyper growth of government that we see today—and the resulting potential for abuse of power—stems from an obscure civil service rule that didn't always exist.

Before the twentieth century, federal employees served at the pleasure of the president. No federal employee had anything like a permanent claim on the public treasury.

Most federal employees did not retain their job past the term of the president they served; in those days, there was no expectation that they would serve for life.

Today, federal employees are presumed to enjoy permanent tenure, regardless of the political climate and regardless of performance.

And permanent tenure is a privilege that gives rise to many other privileges.

Since federal employees are almost impossible to fire, there's little to deter them from infringing your rights.

And there's little to dissuade them from exceeding their authority in countless small yet obnoxious ways.

Permanent tenure lies at the very root of the out-of-control bureaucracy we see today, because it makes public employees immune to rule of law, and subjects them only to orders from on high.

* * *

To discover the origins of the permanent bureaucracy we have today, it's important to demystify the context in which it developed.

The history of the federal civil service can be divided into four periods. Each period is characterized by a different system. There was the Formative System that prevailed from 1789 until 1829; the Spoils System from 1829 to 1883; the Merit System from 1883 to 1912; and the Modern Spoils System that we've had since 1912.

Each of these periods is defined by changes to the rules for hiring and firing federal employees.

The controlling factor in each transformation of the system was a change in the presidential removal power.

Prior to 1912, for example, federal employees had no statutory privilege of permanent tenure.

Incoming presidents, upon entering office, were expected to fire tens of thousands of federal workers.

Although we may find fault with this policy today, it had a number of salutary effects that are worth noting.

First, it kept the size and role of government in check.

Second, it kept the official privileges and insularity of federal employees to a minimum.

Lastly, it kept federal employees from developing their own institutional imperatives, which are always found to be at odds with the interests of ordinary citizens.

The overall effect of mass removals was to hinder the growth of a Prussian-style permanent bureaucracy.

But around the turn of twentieth century, civil service reforms began to prohibit removals altogether.

Thus the modern, overgrown, federal bureaucracy owes its development to subtle changes made to the presidential removal power.

* * *

While the Constitution is clear in its provision for appointments, it says nothing about the removal power.

The Constitution carefully divides the appointment power between the president and the Senate, but it leaves the location of the removal power unspecified.

Not only is the removal power not *mentioned*, but also there's not even the slightest *hint* as to where the framers intended the removal power to reside.

In fact, the location of the removal power may well be the most important structural question the Constitution does not address.

The mystery thickens even further when you discover that the topic of the removal power seems not to have even been discussed at the Federal Convention.

This staggering omission from the Constitution seems to have gone unnoticed until the First Congress, when it came time to create the original executive departments.

Because of the Constitution's silence, the decisions of the First Congress have unique authority among the many precedents which define the removal power today.

* * *

James Madison played a central role in forming the Constitution; and he would play a central role in constituting the presidential removal power as well.

The struggle over the removal power began during the First Congress when Madison introduced a bill to establish the Department of Foreign Affairs.

Madison's bill proposed to give presidents an unrestricted power to remove the secretary of state. This part of the bill became the subject of fierce debate.

Madison's proposal proved especially controversial in the Senate, where the issue of where to vest the removal power had great bearing on senatorial prerogatives.

Because of the Senate's role in confirming presidential appointments, many senators assumed the Senate would have the power to veto removals.

But after several days of inside maneuvering, the question was finally brought to a vote.

And the advocates of a senatorial veto on removals were found to have lost.

The Senate was so closely divided over the issue that the vote was decided only when Vice President John Adams cast the tie-breaking vote.

Senator William Maclay of Pennsylvania later offered an account of the intense passions around the vote:

> I was never treated with less respect than this day.
> Adams behaved with studied inattention...talking
> and sniggering...the whole time I was up.[1]

Maclay's bitterness suggests the high-stakes involved in a vote that became one of the most important precedents in American constitutional history.

The Senate's vote that day became known as the Decision of 1789; and the Decision of 1789 continues to exert controlling influence on our political system over two hundred years later.

Imagine, for example, how differently our political process would work if the president had to win approval from the Senate to remove high-level appointees.

From cabinet officers down to the lowest ranks, power and responsibility would be conflicted and divided under such arrangements.

From this standpoint, the Decision of 1789 was not merely a vote taken by Congress, but a settlement that reinforced the natural order of our Constitution.

The Supreme Court has upheld the Decision of 1789 on several occasions.[2]

In 1868, the Senate also upheld the Decision of 1789 when it acquitted President Andrew Johnson of violating the Tenure of Office Act.[3]

The Decision of 1789 has stood the test of time because the precedent it established was so fundamentally sound—and so consistent with the logic of our Constitution.

* * *

Although the location of the removal power was settled by the Decision of 1789, the use of the removal power remained dormant during the early years of our Republic.

It took the election of Andrew Jackson before any vigorous exercise of the removal power was carried out.

Jackson's exercise of the removal power was a kind of operational test for the Decision of 1789.

Prior to Jackson's election, rotation in office was well-regarded in principle, but more often associated with elective than with administrative offices.

In the meantime, the record of the civil list shows that sons were inheriting offices from their fathers, a practice the public increasingly viewed with disgust.

There was a growing concern that federal civil servants were becoming a separate class, not unlike the functionaries that ruled European countries at the time.

It was against this setting that Jackson entered office, vowing in his first annual message to "destroy the idea of property now so generally connected with official station…by promoting that rotation which constitutes a leading principle in the republican creed."[4]

With this hint at the mass removals to come, Jackson threw open the civil list, and soon began replacing incumbent civil servants with his political supporters.

The practice of removing officeholders and rewarding supporters with jobs became known as the Spoils System, after the maxim, "to the victor belong the spoils."[5]

Although Jackson's removals created a stir, his policy was mild in comparison to the mass removals that would take place under later administrations.

Jackson's policy was also harmless in comparison to the Modern Spoils System, which concentrates power around regulatory czars and White House staffers who are neither vetted nor confirmed by the Senate.

As the Spoils System evolved into an expectation, those who succeeded Jackson in the presidency would push the system much further.

During the Civil War, Lincoln used his patronage power, enlarged by the increase of federal offices, to reward his supporters and advance the war effort.

As historian Carl Fish later observed of Lincoln's practices:

> If Lincoln had made appointments for merit only, the war might have been shortened; on the other hand, he might not have preserved a united North to carry on the war.[6]

The downside of the spoils system, especially with the huge increase of federal offices during the War, was that the spoils were becoming a major burden on presidents.

The point is illustrated by another story about Lincoln, recounted by historian Edward Cary:

In the crisis of the war for the Union [Lincoln] was visited by a committee of New York politicians, intent on patronage. The chairman opened his address with a reference to the 'awful burden of the nation's fate' weighing on the President. "Gentlemen," interrupted Mr. Lincoln, "it is not the fate of the nation that worries me most just now; it is your pesky post office."[7]

Under the vicious cycle of demands to fire and rehire an ever-larger share of the federal administration, the spoils were becoming a nightmare for presidents.

* * *

The Spoils System was becoming a threat to the safety of presidents as well, as evidenced by the assassination of James Garfield in 1881.

Conventional wisdom holds that Garfield's assassin was a "disappointed office-seeker," but there are also indications that he was simply insane.

In any case, the assassination hints at a rising sense of entitlement among party workers—an attitude of inflated expectations that the system could not fulfill.

The shock of the assassination led directly to the passage of the Civil Service Act of 1883[8]—a law that would slowly transform our entire political system.

The Civil Service Act was to provide a formal hiring process for the vast number of government employees whose positions were not subject to Senate confirmation.

There were two positive aspects of the Civil Service Act that are especially worth noting.

First, the Act did not apply to specific offices. Instead, it created a merit system that presidents were authorized to apply at their discretion, by executive order.

Second, the Act provided a framework to regulate only the *hiring* of civil servants, not the *firing*.

The Act said nothing about the presidential removal power, nor was it intended to restrict the removal power.

This second point is especially important not only in light of the precedent set by the Decision of 1789, but also in light of developments that would occur afterward.

The Civil Service Act created the Merit System to reign in the patronage power and tame the spoils.

And it was the truest merit system we've ever had.

The basic idea of the Merit System was to use competitive exams to vet job candidates, in order to reduce patronage as a factor in the hiring decision.

Like the Constitution itself, the Civil Service Act regulated appointments, said nothing of removals, and left the removal power unfettered.

But unlike the Constitution, the Civil Service Act's lack of restriction on the removal power was intentional.

The reformers believed that if the hiring process were properly regulated, then that regulation alone would greatly reduce, if not eliminate, unjust firings.

Regarding the original intent of the Civil Service Act, historian Paul Van Riper would later write:

> the original civil service reformers…consistently fought against an overly absolute tenure as undesirable and unnecessary for civil service reform.[9]

Although the original Civil Service Act did not restrict the removal power, it nonetheless brought an end to the Spoils System.

The reason was simple: the Spoils System had more to do with rewarding political supporters than with arbitrarily punishing incumbent officeholders.

Mass removals were merely a means to an end.

As the Merit System was extended and applied to a larger share of federal offices, the incentive to conduct mass removals was greatly reduced, if not eliminated.

* * *

As the Merit System was expanded to cover a greater number of offices, it became a boon to the presidency.

The Merit System began to restore the strength of the presidency, which was at an all-time low, by delivering presidents from having to dole out offices to spoilsmen.

The Merit System offered such relief to the presidency that presidents expanded the system, by executive order, at a rapid pace.

Within just a few decades, mass removals were no longer conducted despite the Civil Service Act's lack of restriction on the removal power.

The spoils ceased because the *incentive* to conduct mass removals had been largely eliminated.

In other words, the spoils ceased because the Merit System would not allow political bosses to decide who would be hired to replace the workers that were fired.

Every person hired under the Merit System had to be eligible, and their eligibility did not depend on political favor: they became eligible only by taking a competitive exam and scoring in the top tier of applicants.

This restriction in the hiring process eliminated the main reason mass removals were conducted in the first place. It also created such a huge backlog in the hiring process that mass removals became impractical.

Many people at the time viewed mass removals as the worst evil of the Spoils System.

Remarkably, the Merit System ended mass removals, along with the spoils hiring of civil servants—*even though it left the removal power unfettered.*

Instead of restricting the removal power, the Merit System successfully ended mass removals by *regulating the appointment process.*

* * *

Given the success of the Merit System in ending the spoils, it's a little mysterious as to why the Merit System, in its original form, was later abandoned.

The first breach of the Merit System occurred when President William McKinley issued an executive order in 1897, which read:

> No removal shall be made from any position subject to competitive examination except for just cause and upon written charges filed with the head of the Department, or other appointing officer, and of which the accused shall have full notice and an opportunity to make defense.[10]

This 46-word executive order was revolutionary in its ramifications.

Under the order, Merit System appointees no longer served at the pleasure of the president, as they had since Jackson's presidency. Instead, civil servants covered by the Merit System could now be removed only for cause.

The executive order imposed a subtle restriction on the removal power that made it difficult or impossible to conduct any removal to rid the service of incompetent, inefficient, or uncooperative workers.

The executive order entangled the removal power in a burdensome process of hearings and appeals.

The exercise of the removal power now required so much effort that soon, no removals were made.

With the burden of proof for the exercise of the removal power turned on its head, a transformation began to unfold within our system of self-government.

Even Theodore Roosevelt, who had served as a U.S. Civil Service Commissioner in the early 1890s, found McKinley's executive order so repugnant to the original intent of the Merit System that he reversed the order after he became president, in 1902.[11]

In 1912, however, well after Roosevelt had left office, and after heavy lobbying by federal employees and by trade unions, Congress passed the Lloyd-LaFollette Act.[12]

The Lloyd-LaFollette Act not only restricted the presidential removal power, but also granted federal employees the privilege of unionizing for the first time.

The restriction of the removal power brought about a fundamental shift in the relationship between government employees and the American people.

Restriction of the removal power began to erect government employees into a separate and distinct class.

Restriction of the removal power fostered a distinction between "government" and "governed" in America, a country where no such distinction had existed before.

The shift in the reality of American governance caused us to turn away from the tenets of our self-government.

Instead of government of, by and for the people, we now have government that doles out benefits to the people, without constitutional or natural limit.

* * *

In the past century, our concept of governance in America has been transformed, as many have come to accept the belief that government can do for the people what the people cannot do for themselves.

Americans used to be vigilant toward the possibility of tyranny taking root within our own soil.

Since 1912, however, the watchword has been "government *efficiency*," and people have become stunningly complacent toward the danger of government *power*.

Today, we maintain a vast executive branch system that could not have existed under the Jacksonian policy of rotation in office.

The bureaucratic machinery allows presidents of both parties to substitute their will for rule of law and to govern by fiat—via executive order.

In the 1940s, presidential scholar Edward Corwin looked at "the growth of presidential participation in legislation" and wondered whether the presidency had become a "potential matrix of dictatorship."[13]

Corwin's question suggests how far we'd already departed from the principles of self-government, even in his day. Since then, the problem has only grown worse.

The Merit System was supposed to curb the patronage hiring of federal employees.

But we abandoned the Merit System and replaced it with a kind of Modern Spoils System.

Today, government employees can't be fired.

At the same time, we have regulatory czars, recess appointees, and White House staffers who wield enormous power—many of whom assume office without vetting or confirmation by the Senate.

The original constitutional principle was to ensure the *proper vetting* of appointees and to leave the removal power *unfettered*.

Today, the *checks* that properly apply to appointments have been *improperly* applied to *removals*, while the *lack of restraint* that properly applies to removals has been *improperly* applied to appointments. *This is a complete inversion of the original constitutional principle.*

Today, amidst signs and wonders that government has run amok in its abuse of power, we face a choice.

We can restore the unfettered removal power—*along with the due and proper vetting of all high-level presidential appointees*—and thus return our system to the safe harbor of constitutional principle.

Or we can sit back and watch as a "potential matrix of dictatorship" becomes an undeniable and living reality.

11

The Growth of Legislative Blackmail

Today, no practice of any legislature in the world is more debated than the U.S. Senate filibuster.

As politics have become more polarized in the United States, the use of the filibuster has intensified.

Today, nearly every decision of Congress is affected by actual or threatened obstruction in the U.S. Senate.

Meanwhile, critics of the filibuster point to the potential harm done by its use or threatened use.

Because of the way the filibuster is used, the Senate no longer serves as the constitutional check that it once did.

At one extreme, there is a growing number who believe the Senate should be governed under simple majority rule.

At the other, there are those who would place no limit on senators' power to obstruct the business of Congress.

Between these extremes is a truth about the filibuster that is often overlooked today.

Despite its failings, the filibuster serves in its own way to protect minority rights and civil liberties.

The filibuster places the U.S. Senate in a unique role that cannot be fulfilled by the president, by the House of Representatives, or even by the courts.

Distinguishing the legitimate use of the filibuster from so many demagogic, corrupt, and selfish abuses of the filibuster is no easy endeavor.

Still, the question we need to ask is not, "why should we abolish the filibuster?" But rather, "what can we do to allow the filibuster to be preserved?"

* * *

Omitted from most discussion of the filibuster today is what would be lost if the filibuster were abolished.

The filibuster has been on the verge of abolition for decades now, and there seem to be few—*a minority, one might say*—who favor preserving it.

Yet the consequences of abolishing the filibuster are more extensive than they may seem.

Our entire constitutional system was based on a general protection of minority rights against the primal impulses of the majority.

It may be unfashionable to question unfettered majority rule today, but it's not hard to see the danger of it.

In a situation when the same party controls the presidency and both houses of Congress, the filibuster is the only means the political minority has to defend itself.

Some claim that, in the absence of the Senate filibuster, the courts would step in to protect minority rights; but this claim is based in theory and not fact.

Today, with so many people focused on abolishing the Senate filibuster, very few have bothered to understand how it became so exploited and abused.

* * *

Many critics of the filibuster begin their argument with the fact that the filibuster was neither mentioned in the Constitution nor intended by the framers.

But whatever the framers' opinion might be of the modern Senate filibuster, it's clear that they intended to protect minority rights in the legislative process.

Consistent with that purpose, the Constitution provides that "the Yeas and Nays of the Members of either House on any question shall, at the Desire of one fifth of those Present, be entered on the Journal."[1]

Although this rule did not allow *unlimited debate*, its inclusion in the body of the Constitution speaks to the framers' intent to protect minority rights.

Even if we admit that the Constitution fails to mention the filibuster, the same could be said of any number of "extra-constitutional" practices—like the nominating process, the committee system, and the removal power—which are accepted without question today.

The theory that the filibuster is *contrary* to the Constitution is even less supportable.

The Constitution grants to "Each House" the power to "determine the Rules of its Proceedings."[2] And this power is granted without reservation.

But even to claim the Constitution does not provide for the filibuster is not entirely accurate.

The filibuster, after all, did not emerge in a vacuum; it developed out of the structure of the Senate, and that structure is very much provided by the Constitution.

The aspect of the Constitution that has an effect similar to the filibuster is the apportionment of the Senate by states.

The apportionment of the Senate empowers senators representing only a minority of the country to veto legislative acts, even without the filibuster.

But it was the staggered election of senators that truly allowed the filibuster to develop and take root.

Staggered elections provide that only one-third of senators are renewed every two years.

While staggered elections were intended as a bulwark against the "transient impressions"[3] of the majority, they serve another function as well.

Staggered elections make the Senate a continuing body; and this means the Senate majority cannot adopt new rules at the beginning of each new term, as is customary in the House.

Thus staggered elections serve to protect the Senate rules from capricious alteration by the majority, which works to preserve the Senate filibuster even today.

In addition to *staggered* elections, the framers also provided for the *indirect* election of senators. Indirect elections removed the temptation for senators to engage in the kind of grandstanding that's so common today.

It's clear in hindsight that the indirect election of senators served—while it lasted—to moderate the use and temper the abuse of the Senate rules of debate.

The filibuster is often considered in isolation, but it's really a product of the overall structure of the Senate.

* * *

How can we explain the emergence of the Senate filibuster over a hundred-year period, during which the Senate rules of debate did not change?

The filibuster first became *possible* due to the omission of the previous question from the Senate rules.

Under standard parliamentary practice, the previous question gives the majority a way to end debate and bring the pending question to a vote.

The Senate revised its rules in 1806 and eliminated the previous question. In contrast, the rules of the House have admitted the previous question since its inception.[4]

The cloture rule in the modern Senate differs from the previous question, because a cloture vote doesn't *end debate* but rather places a limit on further debate.

The precise reason the previous question was eliminated from the Senate rules is a bit of a mystery.[5]

Even more mysterious—at least from our standpoint today—is that the allowance of unlimited debate existed for decades before senators exploited it.

By most accounts, the *potential* for unlimited debate unleashed by the 1806 Senate rule change did not become *actualized* until 1841, when Senate Democrats tried to stop the passage of a Whig national bank bill.[6]

Even after this first attempt to push the envelope within the Senate rules, the potential for obstruction continued to exist for another *fifty years* before filibustering in the Senate became a regular occurrence.

Even into the 1890s, there were very few senators willing to push the Senate rules to their logical limit.

In other words, even after senators *knew* they could exploit the rules to obstruct Senate business, they mostly refrained from doing so.

This pattern in the rise of the Senate filibuster should cause us to question whether the rise of the modern filibuster owes *at all* to the Senate rules.

* * *

In its early development, the filibuster often appeared as endless debate without any declared intent by the filibusterers to defeat a particular bill.

The practice of filibustering in the Senate first began to resemble the modern filibuster in the 1890s.

In 1897, Senator Matthew Quay of Pennsylvania attempted to amend a bill so as to raise the price the Navy would pay for armor plate.

His reason for the amendment was that it was, "in the interest of millions of Pennsylvania capital and the wages of thousands of Pennsylvania workingmen."[7]

Quay ended up filibustering in the effort to see his amendment pass.

Thus Quay's filibuster marked the first *extortionate* use of unlimited debate.

Although Quay failed, his failure can be attributed to a lack of audacity more than to any other cause: he ended the filibuster under pressure from his Senate colleagues.

Quay was the first to exploit the Senate rules in such a brazen manner, but he would not be the last.

Those who followed in Quay's footsteps would prove far less willing to yield. In fact, later filibusterers would make Quay's filibuster look like the work of an amateur.

In 1903, Senator Ben Tillman of South Carolina picked up where Quay had left off.

The story of Tillman's precedent-shattering filibuster is recounted by historian Frank Burdette:

> On the night of March 3, 1903 [just before the end of the session]…'Pitchfork Ben' Tillman of South Carolina demanded that a claim of some $47,000 for expenses incurred during the War of 1812 be included for his state…Mr. Tillman privately offered to defeat all legislation before the Senate by

reading and talking till adjournment the next day. But Senators had no wish to test the endurance of the South Carolinian, and the item became a part of the bill.[8]

Speaker of the House Joe Cannon called Tillman's action "legislative blackmail."[9]

We can see in hindsight that Tillman was at the vanguard of a new breed of senators who had no scruple about invoking the filibuster for "blackmail" purposes.

Tillman's career, in fact, points to the larger pressures that were beginning to bear on the Senate—pressures that would only intensify the use of the filibuster.

South Carolina was among the first states to adopt the direct primary; and Tillman's "peerless gift of popular appeals"[10] equipped him for success under the new system of direct nomination.

We might even say that Tillman's shameless use of the filibuster was an outgrowth of the populist style that had propelled him to high office under the direct primary.

Tillman was not alone in his grandstanding abuse of the Senate rules.

In 1908, Senator Robert LaFollette of Wisconsin led a filibuster in an attempt to stop the Aldrich-Vreeland Currency Bill from becoming law.

As Frank Burdette would later recount, the Currency Bill was viewed by many as "only another scheme of the money power, an attempt of the privileged few to tighten their grip upon the capital and credit of the country."[11]

Although LaFollette shattered all records by holding the floor for 18 hours, the filibuster was defeated when one of his compatriots mistakenly yielded the floor.

The Currency Bill filibuster is noteworthy not only because of its length, or because of the reinterpretation of the Senate rules that resulted. Its real significance lies in the shift in tactics it reveals: namely, the use of obstruction—rather than coalition building—as an acceptable means of opposing legislation.

LaFollette's strategy for defeating the bill was an outgrowth of his approach to politics. His populism stirred passions, but it often yielded more publicity than efficacy—and more idle applause than sound policy.

Like Tillman, LaFollette was a product of the direct primary. In fact, he was one of the original proponents of the direct primary in his home state of Wisconsin.

LaFollette would have been a very different kind of senator—or he *never* would have been *elected*—were it not for the establishment of the direct primary system.

* * *

Is it a coincidence that so many early adopters of the modern Senate filibuster were senators from states at the vanguard of the direct primary reform movement?

The influence direct elections exerted on the proceedings of the Senate—and the pressure direct elections brought upon the Senate—are well known.

Yet even prior to the establishment of direct elections for the Senate, some three-quarters of the states were already nominating senators by direct primary.[12]

The pressures this created—pressures brought by the *direct primary*, not by *direct election*—seem to explain the rise of the modern filibuster in its early years, before the adoption of the Seventeenth Amendment.

Once the Seventeenth Amendment was adopted—making direct election the rule throughout the country—the frequency and intensity of filibustering exploded.

The number of filibusters in 1913 and 1914—immediately after the adoption of direct elections—was unprecedented.

The story of how direct election affected senators' desire to exploit their right of unlimited debate is worth investigating in far greater detail.

What we do know is that the Senate rules of debate did not change during this period *or at any point after 1806.*

Thus changes to the Senate rules *cannot* account for the growing use and rising intensity of the filibuster.

Among the *likely* causes for the rising use of the filibuster were changes to the mode of nomination and election, occurring right around the same time.

* * *

A few years after the direct election of senators became the law of the land, the stage was set for the "filibuster to end all filibusters" to occur.

This was the Armed Ship Bill filibuster, named for a bill introduced by President Woodrow Wilson to arm merchant vessels in defense against German U-boats.

The contending passions around the Armed Ship Bill testified to the vital question of war and peace at stake in the passage of the bill.

But there was also another cleavage which divided the many opponents of the Armed Ship Bill.

The question that divided the bill's opponents was how to best and most responsibly oppose a bill which many senators believed would draw America into war.

There were a large number of senators who opposed the bill, but who refused to filibuster against it.

What was the difference between the senators who filibustered the bill, and the senators who opposed the bill but refused to filibuster?

The difference seemed to lie in their style of appeal and in their beliefs as to the efficacy of the filibuster as a means of opposing the bill.

What's interesting about the Armed Ship Bill filibuster is that it was led *exclusively* by senators who owed their political careers to direct primary election.

We've already mentioned Robert LaFollette, whose populism was well known and who played a major role in the adoption of the direct primary in Wisconsin.

Moses Clapp of Minnesota was the most senior of the Armed Ship Bill filibusterers. Although originally elected to the Senate under the old mode of nomination and election, Clapp was a fierce advocate for the adoption of the direct primary in his home state.

Albert Cummins of Iowa had pushed his state to adopt the direct primary in 1907 while he was governor. In 1908, he was elected to the Senate after being nominated by direct primary.

James Vardaman of Mississippi was among the most colorful of the Armed Ship Bill filibusterers. Vardaman's temperament and political career bore a number of similarities to Tillman's, including his rabid race-baiting tendencies. Twice denied the gubernatorial nomination at state party conventions, Vardaman began promoting direct primary reform, got his bill passed in 1902, and was elected in 1903. Few careers better exhibit the extent to which the party convention system had hindered demagogues from reaching high office.

While these four were not the only Armed Ship Bill filibusterers, they were among the most prominent and outspoken leaders of the filibuster.

Although seventy-five senators signed a statement supporting the Armed Ship Bill, the session of Congress expired before the Senate could actually vote on the bill.

After the session was adjourned, President Wilson issued a statement denouncing the "little group of willful men"[13] who had obstructed the Armed Ship Bill.

After making his appeal to public opinion, Wilson called the Senate into special session for the express purpose of changing the Senate rules.

After six hours of debate, the Senate adopted Rule 22, the first cloture rule in the history of Congress.

The original Senate cloture rule provided for the limitation of debate after a two-thirds vote of senators present and voting.

This brought to a close the long era of Senate history during which the right of unlimited debate was checked only by a senator's own judgment and self-restraint.

But even the enactment of the cloture rule did not end the discredit of the Armed Ship Bill filibusterers.

Instead of attempting again, during the new session, to seek authorization from Congress, President Wilson instead found an old statute, already on the books, which he used to authorize the very same arming of merchant vessels that Congress had declined to approve.

* * *

Despite the creation of the cloture rule, the Armed Ship Bill episode was only the first of many filibusters that have grown increasingly problematic to say the least.

Today, the filibuster is such a hindrance to the performance of the Senate that it compromises the Senate's power to act as a check against the executive.

Executive agreements signed on the sole authority of the president—without the advice or consent of the Senate—far outweigh, in number and importance, the treaties ratified or otherwise seen by the Senate.

During the Senate's first one hundred years, the United States became a party to 275 treaties and 265 executive agreements. But in the *last fifty years*, the United States became a party to 224 treaties and *3364* executive agreements.[14]

While these numbers *quantitatively* demonstrate the effect of Senate dysfunction on the distribution of power, the reality behind the numbers is even more alarming.

As Senator William Fulbright, longtime chairman of the Senate Foreign Relations Committee, observed during the 1970s:

> We get many treaties dealing with postal affairs and so on. Recently, we had an extraordinary treaty dealing with the protection of stolen art objects. These are treaties. But when we put troops and take on commitments in Spain, it is an executive agreement.[15]

There are a number of ways Congress could rein in the use of executive agreements. For example, Congress could refuse to fund the enforcement of international agreements that haven't been ratified by the Senate.

That Congress declines to take such action *hints* at the larger dimensions of the problem.

As if the abdication of the treaty power weren't enough, the same problem can be seen in the area of executive appointments.

Regulatory czars appointed unilaterally by the president, without the advice or consent of the Senate, are an increasing share of all appointments made today.

While the number of "czars" is not huge—there have been around thirty during the Bush and Obama years so far—these unconfirmed "czars" wield enormous power.

And czars appointed by sole authority of the president were practically nonexistent before the Clinton years.

Recess appointments to the executive and judicial branches—which also, in effect, bypass the Senate—have increased at the same time.

While other factors may be afoot, it would be hard to argue the filibuster is *not* a factor in this overall trend.

* * *

Given the Senate's neglect of its executive duties, it's fair to ask whether the filibuster is really worth keeping.

But when it comes to weighing the outright abolition of the filibuster, it's crucial to consider the protection of minority rights the filibuster provides.

The existence of the Senate filibuster is never more crucial than at those times when the majority controls the presidency along with both chambers of Congress.

This is also when the filibuster is most exposed and liable to elimination.

Staggered elections make the Senate a continuing body under parliamentary law, but the Senate's *actual status* as a continuing body remains a matter of interpretation.

The Vice President, acting as president of the Senate, can at any time, with the approval of the majority, issue a ruling from the chair that would in effect abolish the filibuster.

And the much-threatened use of this so-called "nuclear" option has never been more imminent.

The Senate's action in November of 2013 to curb the filibuster is proof of the threat the filibuster faces today. While the Senate's action stopped short of ending the filibuster outright, it did end the filibuster for executive and judicial appointments, excepting appointments to the Supreme Court.

The Senate did not go further and end the filibuster, because even the majority of that moment recognized that such a step would be irreversible.

But the incident raises a larger question: is the filibuster really the problem, or is it merely a symptom of the broader dysfunction of Congress?

* * *

As the history of the Senate shows, the Senate rules have remained constant for long periods, even while norms around the use of the rules changed dramatically.

If abuse of the Senate filibuster has become extreme and even obscene, it is but a reflection of how extreme the Senate itself has become.

Distracted by the same issues that preoccupy every other legislature in the United States, the U.S. Senate has ventured so far from its original practice that the framers would hardly recognize it today.

The framers of the Constitution provided the indirect election of senators to prevent the kind of grandstanding and chest thumping that we take for granted in the normal course of Senate proceedings today.

As with the rest of government, the temper of the Senate stems from the mode of nomination.

No change to the Senate rules will ever to compensate for the damage done by the present mode of nomination.

Viewing the problem in scientific terms, abuse of the filibuster is not an effect of the Senate rules, but of the mode of nomination.

Like so many practices that are tearing our republican institutions apart at the seams, a more-than-fleeting look at the filibuster reveals it is a symptom and not the cause.

Like so much of the chaos in our political process today, the modern filibuster sprang from the direct primary: that trial by ordeal which all candidates must undergo, prior to their admission to the seat of power.

12

The Transformation of the Money Power

Never in the history of the world were the economic destinies of so many in the hands of so few, as today under the monetary system of the Federal Reserve.

The policies of the Federal Reserve are made by a tiny cabal of supposed experts whose decisions are in no way subject to rule of law or outside scrutiny.

Federal Reserve policies are not only contrary to free market principles; the policies have caused a breakdown of honest money—and honest dealings—throughout our economy.

The Fed has destroyed entire productive industries through its inflationary policies; and it's destroying the American middle class, right now, in the exact same way.

Today, the Fed stands committed to printing money indefinitely under the pretense of promoting "economic recovery" from a financial crisis of its own creation.

But the real intent of its policy is to bailout insolvent banks; and the real effect of its policy is to make the rich richer, the poor poorer, and the middle nonexistent.

Even though many people see through the elaborate lies used to justify Fed policies, the damage being done by those policies is far greater than most people realize.

The consequences of the Fed's present policies are written in the lessons of history.

Incessant money printing can only lead to the collapse of the currency, to the breakdown of supply chains, and to the suspension or loss of our republican institutions.

Because the worst case scenario is already playing out, it's important for people to understand not only what is happening, but what can be done about it as well.

* * *

Amidst the fear of an impending monetary disaster, there's a staggering lack of vision among those who advocate alternatives to the present system.

Even among the Fed's critics, many commentators fail to account for the real reason why Fed policies continue to unfold as they do.

Many people promote the theory that the Fed is merely a tool of private financial interests. While this may be true, the Fed can be better understood as a *political animal*—and as a component of our *political institutions.*

By viewing the Federal Reserve as a political creature—and *not* as a private bank—we can begin to uncover the real reason why the Fed exists.

If the Fed is considered in light of its political aspect, its main function is not to make the rich richer, although that is certainly a major effect of its policies.

Rather, the main function of the Fed—as a creature of the political system—is to fund the profligate spending and endless deficits of the central government.

Viewing the Fed in this light not only brings us closer to the way of thinking that's needed to "End the Fed."

This perspective also clearly reveals the universal danger that arises from endless deficit spending.

The Fed's existence as a political creature reveals the codependence that *always develops* between insolvent governments and private banking establishments.

* * *

The best way to think about the political problem posed by the Federal Reserve is to call to mind the age-old dichotomy between rule of law and the will of men.

The monetary system of our Constitution was supposed to govern currency fluctuations under rule of law, thus placing the standard of exchange beyond the reach of men.

Today, however, we entrust our medium of exchange entirely to the fallible discretion of a chosen few, thus placing our entire economy at the mercy of their error-prone judgment.

The monetary system of our Constitution was supposed to end political control of the currency.

Today, however, we allow a tiny central committee to manipulate the standard of value which is most widely accepted throughout our economy.

The monetary system of our Constitution was supposed to be automatically self-stabilizing under fixed rules, and ultimately controlled by supply and demand.

Today, however, we allow the Fed's monetary mandarins to indulge in their own kind of irrational exuberance, which subjects our economy to a boom and bust cycle of continuous bubbles and panics.

The monetary system of our Constitution was supposed to undergird rule of law and economic prosperity with sound money.

Today, however, half of every transaction in our economy—the monetary half—is settled by a medium of exchange that is increasingly lawless, and which undermines rule of law and economic freedom.

The monetary system of our Constitution was so simple that just about anyone could understand it.

Today, however, we find ourselves debating delicate questions of "monetary policy"—*how many tens of billions of money should the Fed print in a given month?*—questions which wouldn't even exist under a monetary system governed under rule of law.

From the perspective of history, the monetary situation in which we find ourselves today is bizarre.

Today, the Fed has co-opted economic discourse to such a degree—with continuous speeches, policy communications, and confabs—that we find ourselves debating personnel and policies, when we should really be debating the existence of the Federal Reserve itself.

* * *

When the Federal Reserve was established in 1913, it was not the first central bank that had been planted in American soil.

But it was the first central bank chartered in perpetuity, and this fact is important for several reasons.

The two earlier efforts to introduce central banking into the American economy were both terminated when Congress refused to renew their corporate charters.

In both cases, the charter expiration and request for renewal were occasions of great debate and careful scrutiny of the banks' performance.

And, in both cases, the central banks failed to measure up and were terminated.

Central bank advocates learned a lesson from this. In their third attempt to deceive the people into accepting an institution so contrary to the public interest, they did not ask for a limited charter that would expire.

Instead, they depicted the proposed central bank as just another agency of government; and, as such, it was only sensible for the bank to be established in perpetuity.

Prior to the formation of the Fed, our monetary system was a subject of continuous debate and an object of intense struggle.

For the most part, the result of that continuous debate was sound money.

Since the formation of the Fed, however, we've mostly taken the monetary system we depend on for granted. This is true of academics, politicians, and citizens alike.

Today, the only debate regarding our monetary system is over whom the next Fed chairman will be. And even that's not a debate; it's more like a foregone conclusion.

This lack of fruitful discussion is becoming dangerous, given the Fed's imminent failure as an institution.

To revive the great monetary debate of our past, with the hope that we might restore sound money, let's begin with a basic outline of our country's monetary history.

The monetary history of the United States can be divided into three major periods: the First Central Banking Era from 1791 to 1832; the Independent Treasury Era from 1832 until 1913; and the Second

Central Banking Era (or Federal Reserve Era) that we find ourselves in today.[1]

These periods could be further subdivided on the basis of changes made to the monetary system during each era; but this simple, threefold division is enough for the historical account that follows.

The Central Banking Eras are characterized by central banking institutions established and authorized to act as fiscal agents for the central government.

The Independent Treasury Era, on the other hand, was marked by a U.S. Treasury empowered to act on its own behalf—really, as its own bank—vaulting and managing its cash balances outside the banking system.

Placing these three periods of American monetary history before us, one very large pattern is evident which demands our attention.

If you took this outline of monetary history and placed it over the history of our political institutions, you would see two very striking coincidences.

Not once, but twice in our history,[2] a major change in our nominating institutions altered the political process enough to also transform the country's monetary system.

That these changes would be related makes sense for two reasons: first, the monetary system is dictated by the funding demands of the central government; and second, those funding demands are driven by the kind of appeals and promises that get politicians elected.

The transition from the First Central Banking Era to the Independent Treasury Era began when Andrew Jackson was elected to the presidency in 1828.

Jackson would not have been elected without the party convention system that enabled his rise to power.

The transition from the Independent Treasury Era to the Federal Reserve Era began when Woodrow Wilson was elected to the presidency in 1912.

Wilson would not have been elected without the direct primary system that clinched his nomination.

The pattern of these major transition points suggests a hidden link between the monetary and the political that is worth exploring at a deeper level.

* * *

Before Andrew Jackson was elected in 1828, presidential selection had been determined by the congressional caucus system of nomination.

Under that system, members of Congress decided the nomination of presidential candidates.

The congressional caucus system was tailor made to foster rule by a small national elite, which is what it did until it fell apart in 1824.

In 1824, Andrew Jackson ran for the presidency without the endorsement of the congressional caucus.

Although he won a plurality of the popular vote, he did not win the Electoral College majority needed to avoid a contingency election in the House.

Jackson was not a party to the "corrupt bargain" that finally settled the election in the House. And so he lost.

Jackson's candidacy may have faltered again in 1828 if the congressional caucus had been assembled.

But Jackson and his supporters did not wait to see what would happen.

Instead, they organized the party convention system that delivered Jackson to the presidency in the election that followed.

And thus the party convention system was the vehicle that allowed the Jacksonian Revolution to take place.

Jackson's plan was to use his influence as president to restore power to the people.

And the continued existence of the Second Bank of the United States was a major mote in the eye of that vision.

The Second Bank, established in 1816 under a twenty-year charter, was mired in scandal, corruption, and cronyism from the very moment it was formed.

Jackson was a sworn enemy of the Bank well before his election to the presidency.

But rather than provoking excitement around the issue, Jackson seemed inclined to let the Bank die a quiet death, by simply allowing its charter to expire.

The showdown between Jackson and the Bank began only when the Bank's President, Nicholas Biddle, started lobbying Congress to renew the Bank's charter in the spring of 1832.

Biddle was requesting the renewal of the charter four years before it was set to expire, so as to make the bank an issue in the presidential election later that year.

After Congress passed the renewal bill, Jackson was presented with the bill on July 4, 1832. He vetoed the bill, he said, "with solemn regard to the principles of the Constitution which the day was calculated to inspire."[3]

With the gauntlet thus thrown down, Biddle used every lever of influence at his disposal to defeat Jackson's reelection bid.

Biddle's electioneering included funding Jackson's opponent Henry Clay, giving loans to members of Congress, and manipulating the credit conditions of the country.

When Clay lost the election, it was clear the Bank was doomed.

Although Jackson had been inclined to let the Bank's charter expire peaceably, the election changed his view.

Shortly after his reelection, Jackson ordered the removal of government deposits from the Bank, which practically forced the Bank to cease operations.

Jackson's action against the Bank was so controversial that it continued to excite spirited debate decades later.

In all likelihood, the termination of the Bank would not have taken palace as it did, if any person with less firmness and resolve were president at the time.

Jackson's temperament no doubt stemmed from his experiences, but his temperament made its way to the presidency through the party convention system.

* * *

One major legacy of the Jacksonian Revolution was an enduring political consensus in favor of sound money.

The sound money consensus seemed to arise in tandem with the spread of the party convention system of nomination.

The Jacksonian Period witnessed the rise of many national figures whose views on money would make them pariahs in our political process today.

Senator Thomas Hart Benton of Missouri was the architect of the Coinage Act of 1834. Benton believed:

> Gold and silver are the best currency for a republic; it suits the men of middle property and the working people best; and if I was going to establish a workingman's party it should be on the basis of hard money.[4]

Martin Van Buren was the mastermind who had engineered the formation of the party convention system on Andrew Jackson's behalf in 1828.

Later, as president, Van Buren secured the passage of the country's first independent treasury act, in an effort to deliver the U.S. Treasury from the private banking system. He believed central banking institutions to be inherently harmful to the interests of ordinary people.

In 1844, James K. Polk was selected as the first "dark horse" presidential candidate, largely due to his view on the "bank question."[5] If today's presidential nominating process was in place then, Polk would not have been nominated, even though he was highly qualified.

As president, Polk established the Independent Treasury System: the arrangement that most closely adhered to the monetary principles of our Constitution, out of all the monetary systems we've ever had.[6]

Unfortunately, the Jacksonian consensus in favor of sound money was suspended—along with specie payments from the U.S. Treasury—during the massive deficit spending of the Civil War.

It was during the Civil War that Congress erected the National Banking System on top of the Independent Treasury System, thus displacing hard money reserves with national debt and national banknotes (which became reserves under the National Banking System).

By providing a national currency backed by government debt, the National Banking System severed the link between hard money reserves and the quantity of money and credit in circulation. This removed the restraints on money and credit creation that had existed under the pure Independent Treasury System.

Under the National Banking System, fiscal deficits would stimulate and expand the creation of bank credit. In contrast, under the Independent Treasury, deficit spending tended to hamper and restrict the creation of bank credit; and this had served to moderate the boom and bust cycle in a countercyclical manner.[7]

Also under the National Banking System—with the creation of bank credit divorced from any strict requirement for banks to hold hard money reserves—private "money center" banks secured a privileged position to control credit conditions throughout the economy.

The concentrated influence of the national banks made the financial system unstable, which caused the U.S. Treasury to intervene in the money market.

While the Treasury's moves were supposed to provide "seasonal elasticity" to the currency, the interventions actually made the banking system *more* unstable.

Because the National Banking System was increasingly prone to euphoric booms and violent busts—and also because the fiscal surpluses of the U.S. government were causing long-term price deflation—the monetary system was becoming embroiled in political controversy toward the end of the nineteenth century.

In 1896, the Democratic Party platform proposed restoring the free coinage of silver; and Democratic presidential candidate William Jennings Bryan decried the "cross of gold" that was crucifying the prosperity of ordinary people. While Bryan's free silver plan is often depicted as radical or inflationist, it would have merely restored the original, silver-based U.S. monetary system.

But Bryan was demonized and he lost the election.

Bryan ran on a similar platform in 1900, and was defeated once again by William McKinley.

Just before the election, McKinley oversaw the passage of the Gold Standard Act, which placed the United States on the international gold standard for the first time.

With fervor around the "money question" running at such a fever pitch, it's natural that the debate was not confined to the consideration of gold and silver only.

In 1901, the American Socialist party was formed with the avowed aim of establishing "public ownership of the means of exchange." This plank of the Socialist platform was later clarified to demand "the collective ownership and democratic management of the banking and currency system."[8]

But the Socialists were outside the mainstream of the great monetary debate that was taking place.

The general consensus still favored a monetary system backed by precious metals in some form.

Remarkably, in the space of a decade, the mainstream consensus—so seemingly disdainful toward *even the idea* of unbacked paper money—would be turned on its head.

* * *

In accounting for the rapid demise of the classical gold standard in favor of a Fed-managed gold exchange standard, many historians point to the Panic of 1907.

Often, the Gold Standard Act of 1900 is blamed for the severity of the panic that occurred in 1907.[9]

While it's true that the Panic was aggravated by gold outflows to England during the crisis, it's also true that the Gold Standard Act had increased the leverage of the National Banking System, leaving the system more vulnerable to bank runs.[10]

In addition, the conventional wisdom around the Panic of 1907 fails to account for the economic run up to the crisis: in particular, the trend of erratic deficit spending by the U.S. government, which prompted the gold outflows in the first place.[11]

Thus while the Panic is often blamed on the gold standard, the reason for the severity of the Panic lay in deficit spending, over-leverage, and gold outflows; and the gold outflows were a response to the first two issues.

In any case, the Panic did indeed cause a shift in the monetary consensus, a shift that would transform the entire system within the space of a few years.

In 1908, Congress passed the heavily filibustered Aldrich-Vreeland Currency Act, which allowed banks to issue "emergency currency" during financial panics.

This was followed a few years later by the passage of the Federal Reserve Act at a sparsely attended vote held in Congress on December 23, 1913.

The question of how to explain such a rapid shift in the monetary consensus, within just a few years, is a question of high importance today.

At least one explanation for the monetary shift can be found in the changes to American political institutions that were happening at the same time.

In 1910, the House of Representatives succumbed to mob rule induced by direct primary elections.

In 1913, the Senate was not far behind.

That left only the presidency to stand against the tide of political innovation that was sweeping the country.

But even the presidency proved no match for the direct primary.

Because of the small number of presidential direct primaries held in 1912, you would think the new system merely *influenced* the outcome of the 1912 election.

But because of the way the races within each party unfolded, it would be more accurate to say the direct primary *determined* the outcome of the 1912 election.

On the Republican side, the general election vote was divided between Roosevelt and Taft, largely due to the effects of the direct primaries held earlier that year.

This meant the Democratic nominee—*whoever it happened to be*—would win election by default.

Woodrow Wilson may have seemed like a long-shot nominee in 1912, but he stood a better chance at the Democratic National Convention than is often realized.

For over a year before the convention was set to meet, Wilson had been quietly traveling to primary states and making speeches, openly campaigning for nomination.

As governor, he was instrumental in securing the passage of New Jersey's presidential primary law.

And he had a deep, intuitive grasp of the effects the direct primary would have on the election, and on his prospects for election.

Wilson was among the top two contenders for nomination from the very beginning of the convention.

But the convention remained deadlocked due to the extreme factionalism elicited by the direct primary.

Wilson attained the two-thirds majority he needed to win nomination only after forty-five rounds of balloting.

All of this would *seem* to qualify Wilson as a "dark horse" candidate, if ever there was one.

Wilson's record of public service of all of two years only reinforces this view.

But the fact is this: Wilson would never have even been in the running—*he would not have been considered in the first place*—but for the new system of direct primary election, which enabled his candidacy.

Prone as he was to speak and think in terms of abstract ideology rather than concrete reality, the direct primary was tailor-made for a person like Wilson to get elected to the presidency, for the first time ever.

* * *

Quite the opposite of Wilson—in political outlook and in temperament—was Senator Elihu Root of New York.

Root was among the last of a type of public servant that first came to office during the Jacksonian Era.

Root, like others who shared his worldview, had a deep appreciation of the connection between sound money, political liberty, and economic freedom.

Not coincidentally, Root was also among the last of an era of senators nominated by party convention and elected by legislative appointment.

Having served under presidents McKinley and Roosevelt, Root was elected to the Senate in 1908 and served for one six-year term.

He served in the Senate at the precise moment when the entire system was undergoing its headlong transition from party conventions to direct primary elections.

Root's term in the Senate straddled the point in time when the American political process began to feel the effects of direct primary election.

When Root spoke in opposition to the Federal Reserve Act in December of 1913, days before its passage into law, he represented a dwindling minority that was rapidly vanishing from the American political landscape.

Among the long-range consequences of the Federal Reserve Act, Root predicted:

> Unless our human nature has been changed, we may confidently expect that under this proffer of easy money from a paternal Government, available for each one of us...that the same process will occur that has occurred time and time and time again in older countries.
>
> That process is this...Little by little business is enlarged with easy money. With the exhaustless reservoir of the Government of the United States furnishing easy money, the sales increase, the businesses enlarge, more new enterprises are started, the spirit of optimism pervades the community...
>
> Everyone is making money. Everyone is growing rich...[until] some one whose capacity for business was small, breaks...and down comes the whole structure.
>
> That, sir, is no dream. That is the history of every movement of inflation since the world's business began, and it is the history of many a period in our own country...[this process is what happens] when credit exceeds the legitimate demands of the country...[12]

Thus Root predicted the credit bubble of the 1920s and the Great Depression that followed. His speech also foretold the many other crises that have occurred since the formation of the Federal Reserve, the most recent being the Financial Crisis of 2008.

Root spoke the truth, undaunted by the vague fears of financial panic that were used to pass the Federal

Reserve Act. He was unwilling to indulge the folly and ignorance that were beginning to grip American politics.

Root was among the last of a breed of statesmen who saw clearly what is at stake in the "money question."

He was also among the last willing to speak frankly and honestly on the question, rather than pander to the delusions of monetary mob rule.

Root's honesty extended to other questions as well.

Three years earlier, in opposition to the direct election of senators, Root predicted the effect of the proposed constitutional amendment:

> The time will come when the Government of the United States will be driven to the exercise of more arbitrary and unconsidered power, will be driven to greater concentration, will be driven to extend its functions into the internal affairs of the States... we shall go through the cycle of concentration of power at the center while the States dwindle into insignificance.[13]

Perhaps even more interesting is the connection Root saw between the monetary and the electoral, a connection he hinted at when he accepted his appointment to the Senate in 1909:

> the men who make the most noise about state rights are very apt to be the men who are the most willing and the most desirous to have the national Government step in and usurp the functions of a state when there is an appropriation carried with the usurpation.[14]

Root understood the primal urge of centralized federal authority to draw all power into its orbit—and lay hold of the states—through the exercise of its spending power.

The spending power needed only a lack of restraint—first, by U.S. Senators being made unaccountable to state governments; and second, by the unlimited printing press afforded by the Federal Reserve—and then the spending power, left to its own devices, would yield the extreme concentration of power we see today.

Had Root stood for reelection in 1914, he would have had to canvass the entire state of New York in the general election. He felt neither temperamentally nor politically equipped to campaign in a statewide election.

Thus he declined to run in 1914, and retired from the Senate.

While Root was not typical even in his own day, he was of a type no longer found in our political process.

And the contrast between Woodrow Wilson and Elihu Root could not be more striking.

Wilson celebrated popular rule in the abstract, but betrayed the people in practice.

Root refused to indulge the people with false promises, yet he was their greatest defender in reality.

This paradox is consistent with the strange effects of the direct primary that we've observed throughout this period of history.

The direct primary gives high place to politicians who proclaim themselves friends of the people, but who destroy the people in a thousand undetectable ways.

* * *

The great mystery in the monetary history of the United States is that we once had a system far better than what we have today, yet we abandoned that system.

One of the great myths of our monetary history is that we abandoned the gold standard in 1971, when President

Richard Nixon closed the "gold window" to prevent further redemption of U.S. gold by foreign governments.

In reality, the gold standard was abandoned when the Federal Reserve was formed; and even before *that*, the integrity of the gold standard under the National Banking System was certainly open to question.

To understand the truth that lies at the heart of all of this, we must examine the *system of political institutions* of which the monetary system is but a part.

It's interesting, for example, that the monetary system of the Federal Reserve so closely resembles the regime of philosopher-kings that Woodrow Wilson brought to political power.

It's no secret that Wilson was unapologetically hostile to our constitutional system of checks and balances.

Wilson's entire project, as professor and as president, was to persuade the people to "think less of checks and balances…and more of the synthesis of action."[15]

Wilson's destruction of the very *possibility* of sound money was consistent with his worldview.

Wilson understood—at least intuitively—that sound money was a powerful check against political power.

The economist Ludwig von Mises, writing in 1912, placed sound money "in the same class with political constitutions and bills of rights."[16]

Wilson's destruction of *the very possibility of sound money* was thus a kind of clandestine coup against our system of checks and balances.

While it may be pure coincidence that a person of Wilson's outlook and demeanor waltzed into the presidency the first time the direct primary was used to nominate a president, his ideology and temperament were entirely consistent with the broader effects of the direct primary on our system of checks and balances.

All of this suggests the deep, implicit hostility of our present monetary and political order to the liberties and interests of ordinary people.

Today, we find ourselves at a decisive point in history: we must "end the Fed" before the Fed ends America as we know it.

But the great lesson of our political and monetary history is that we cannot end the Fed without first changing the process we use to nominate candidates.

That is, *we cannot abolish the Fed without first abolishing the direct primary.*

Let us hope we can restore our system of checks and balances—political and monetary—before the forces unleashed by catastrophic inflation destroy our Republic.

13

The Rise of
Government by Judiciary

The modern Supreme Court's judicial activism is proof positive of the extent to which the will of men has trumped rule of law, under our system today.

Judicial activism is taken to signify judges interpreting the law—whether statutory or constitutional—on the basis of their own whims, preferences, and prejudices.

Judicial activism has allowed judges to seize greater power over our legal system, without any legislative authorization whatsoever.

As a result, judicial activism has made appointments to the bench—and to the Supreme Court, in particular— more contentious than at any other time in our history.

But does judicial activism result from the *philosophy* an individual judge or justice might adopt?

What if judicial activism were found to be no different than other forms of government activism, as practiced by the executive and legislative branches?

And what if the primary factor enabling judicial activism were found to lie in the structure of judicial institutions?

Looking at judicial activism this way—as a *lack of checks and balances* and not as *need for better personnel*—the problem becomes straightforward.

In the case of the federal judiciary and Supreme Court, the issue of checks and balances is closely related to the courts' jurisdiction.

And this issue of the courts' jurisdiction is more complicated than it may at first appear.

A look at the history of the Supreme Court reveals a major shift by the Court from passive judging to active policymaking, around a hundred years ago.

The shift was the result of the elimination of checks and balances from the federal judiciary, which brought increased power to the Supreme Court.

Judicial activism was nothing new, even then, but the jurisdictional shift brought the Court into *unprecedented territory*—where it's remained ever since.

* * *

To identify the roots of the modern Supreme Court's activism, it's important that we don't cast too wide a net.

Napoleon famously wanted his judges to be robots, as far as concerned their interpretation of his beloved Code Napoleon.

Today, the Code Napoleon is still the dominant civil law system in the world; but it's not *our* system.

In contrast to the civil law system, our common law system, which originated in England, customarily confers greater authority on precedent, which usually takes the form of judge-made law.

Some people criticize judge-made law as a usurpation of legislative power. Others condemn the doctrine of *stare decisis* that judges use to justify their recourse to precedent. But we should think carefully about these practices before denouncing them too hastily.

Judge-made law is essential to the proper functioning of an independent judiciary.

Judge-made law is also necessary if the judiciary is to act as a check against the legislative and executive power, whenever either branch exceeds its proper authority.

Beyond the issue of judge-made law, others condemn the doctrine of judicial review.

The argument against judicial review is that the federal courts' power to review legislative acts was not provided by the Constitution.

But neither judge-made law nor judicial review would be such a problem if the judicial power were *constituted modestly* and *exercised passively*, as originally intended.

Let's suppose for a moment that we somehow eliminated judge-made law *and* judicial review.

Would that leave us better off?

Or would it merely eliminate two of our most important checks against government power?

In any case, you have to look elsewhere if you want to identify the real cause of the most extreme form of judicial activism today.

With the activism of the modern Supreme Court in view, one factor that's worth examining is the obscure practice known as the writ of certiorari.

Black's Law Dictionary defines the writ of certiorari as:

> An extraordinary writ issued by an appellate court, at its discretion, directing a lower court to deliver the record in the case for review. *The U.S. Supreme Court uses certiorari to review most of the cases it decides to hear* [1]

The writ of certiorari is so powerful because it gives the Supreme Court a discretionary jurisdiction to "decide which cases to decide."

The writ of certiorari is the key to understanding the Court's shift in posture from passive judging to active policymaking, which began around a hundred years ago.

* * *

Even at a glance, it's clear the modern federal judiciary bears little resemblance to the modest federal judiciary created during the early years of our Republic.

When the Constitution was being formed, there were those were those who wanted to create a powerful and energetic central government.

And there were others who wanted to keep most power in the states, and give the federal government only the minimum strength necessary.

The Constitution reflects this tension in a number of areas. And nowhere is this tension more obvious than in the constitutional provisions for the federal judiciary.

On both sides, the federal judiciary was viewed as the crux of the issue—the single most important factor in determining the distribution of state and federal power.

Both sides sought to turn the judicial power to their own purposes.

The result was that Article III of the Constitution— which specifies the form of the federal judiciary— provides only a bare skeletal outline.

So if you want to see what the original federal judiciary looked like, you can't look at the Constitution.

You have to look at the Judiciary Act of 1789.

The Judiciary Act of 1789 enjoys a special place in the history of the federal judiciary not only because it was the *original* judiciary act, but also because several of its authors also helped to write the Constitution itself.

The Judiciary Act of 1789 had three major elements that shaped the early development of the federal courts.[2]

First, it limited the jurisdiction of federal courts by requiring most cases arising under federal law to be tried in state courts, subject to appeal in federal court. The division of jurisdiction was intended to secure a degree of local control over the judicial process.

Second, the Act required Supreme Court justices to ride circuit. Circuit riding required the justices to travel within a "circuit"—or district—to hear cases at the locations where they arose.

Circuit riding was not merely a holdover from earlier customs. It was intended to keep the justices close to local circumstances. While it lasted, it also forced a kind of geographical representation which ensured that the Supreme Court's justices were drawn from every area of the country.

Third, the Act made appeals to the Supreme Court a matter of right, regulated by law.

The framers of the Act probably did not appreciate the importance of this third provision. In fact, this provision can't be truly appreciated without an understanding of the modern Supreme Court's discretionary jurisdiction.

These provisions of the Judiciary Act of 1789 worked in symphony to strike a balance between state and federal power, by restricting the role, influence, and centralizing force of the federal judiciary.

* * *

The federal judicial organization forged by the Judiciary Act of 1789 worked well to keep the Supreme Court in check during its early years.

Some might even say it worked *too* well.

In 1795, Chief Justice of the Supreme Court John Jay resigned in disgust over the Court's lack of influence.

When John Adams tried to reappoint Jay in 1800, Jay declined the offer, citing the Court's want of "energy, weight, and dignity."[3]

Given the Supreme Court's power today, it's hard to imagine any one declining an appointment to the Court. But Adams had a hard time filling the vacancy.

Finally, he prevailed on John Marshall to accept the apparently thankless job of chief justice.

Today, Marshall's tenure as chief justice is widely seen as a turning point for the Court.

But no one knew at the time that the Court would gain such prestige under Marshall's leadership.

It was Marshall's vision and imagination—and not the power of the Court per se—that made the Marshall Court a force to be reckoned with.

Marshall's interpretation of the Court's power was not without controversy; and his ruling in *Marbury v. Madison* is a famous case in point.

Marbury v. Madison was the first ruling in American history in which the Supreme Court struck down a provision of an act of Congress.

Because the Constitution does not give the Court authority to strike down legislative acts—much less acts of Congress—the ruling is still debated even today.

Marshall got away with such a bold assertion of judicial power because the ruling was a masterpiece of subtlety and—ironically—judicial restraint.

In asserting the supremacy of the Supreme Court over the other branches of government, Marshall did so by striking down a section of the Judiciary Act of 1789.

By denying the Court's jurisdiction to hear the case, the ruling actually diminished the Court's power.

But the ruling saved the Court from a political fight that it most assuredly would have lost.

Thus this early instance of judicial review was a far cry from the kind of self-aggrandizing rulings the Court would later engage in, under the guise of judicial review.

* * *

Whatever controversies the Marshall Court may have invited, the early Supreme Court was thoroughly restricted by statutory restraints on its judicial power.

But over time, restraints on the federal judicial power were chipped away.

The first time this happened was in 1833, when South Carolina sought to nullify a tariff law recently enacted by Congress.

Congress's response to the nullification standoff was to pass the Removal Act of 1833.

The Removal Act allowed "any civil suit or criminal prosecution…under…any revenue law of the United States"[4] to be removed from state court into federal court.

At the option of either party, cases involving federal tax laws were now under the jurisdiction of the federal courts. In practice, this meant that federal prosecutors would now try revenue cases in federal court.

During the Civil War and Reconstruction, Congress expanded the removal jurisdiction of the federal courts in its effort to preserve and restore the Union.[5]

CARL JARVIS

Then, long after the crisis had passed, Congress enacted the Removal Act of 1875.[6] The Act gave the parties to any case arising under federal law the option to remove the trial to federal court.

With the passage of the Removal Act of 1875, the balance between state and federal power—so carefully wrought in 1789—was finally overthrown.

* * *

The Removal Act of 1875, along with the Court's new-fangled doctrines, combined to bring about a staggering centralization of the American legal system.

The Fourteenth Amendment was passed to guarantee the civil rights of freed slaves, but soon the Court was using it to strike down state economic regulations that had nothing to do with the rights of freed slaves.

The major effect of these rulings was to expand the jurisdiction—and workload—of the federal courts.

The Removal Act was a boon to railroads and other large corporations that stood to benefit by having their cases tried in federal court, rather than in state court.

During the twenty-year period after 1860, the Supreme Court saw the number of cases on its docket *quadruple* from 310 in 1860 to 1212 in 1880.[7]

While this was happening, the Supreme Court seems not to have questioned the extension of its jurisdiction over state legislative acts previously outside its purview.

By the early 1890s, the Supreme Court was three years behind on its docket, with 1816 cases pending.[8] This was the crisis which brought about the passage of the Judiciary Act of 1891.

The Judiciary Act of 1891 was, first and foremost, a reorganization of the federal courts.

Not only did the Act create an independent tier of circuit courts of appeal. In the same fell swoop, it brought an end to what little had remained of the circuit riding duties of Supreme Court justices.

In creating the circuit courts of appeal, the Act gave the circuit courts final authority to decide most cases.

Among the Act's more obscure provisions, it also gave the losing party in an appeal the right to appeal the ruling to the Supreme Court, by writ of certiorari.

Through this little-noticed provision, the law gave the Court discretion over its docket for the first time, and eliminated litigants' right to appeal as a matter of law.

This shrunk the Court's mandatory jurisdiction and expanded its discretionary appellate jurisdiction.

With this statutory sleight of hand, the Court gained the power to "decide which cases to decide."

Although this change in the Court's appellate jurisdiction was subtle, it marked a watershed in the evolution and development of the Supreme Court.

By using the writ of certiorari to control its docket and caseload, the Court began to transform itself from "passive judge" into "active policymaker."

* * *

While the effects of the writ of certiorari were unfolding, the implications of the "certiorari power" were clearly understood by only a handful of people.

Among those who recognized the power of certiorari to expand the jurisdiction of the Supreme Court—potentially without limit—was William Howard Taft.[9]

After Taft lost his bid for reelection to the presidency in 1912, he lost no time in pursuing his next campaign: he sought not only to become Chief Justice of the

Supreme Court, but also to revolutionize the Court's role in the American political process.

Taft wasn't shy about what he sought to achieve, at least early on. He wanted for the Court to have "absolute and arbitrary discretion"[10] over its docket.

His aim was to shrink the number and type of "mundane" cases the Court was required to hear even below the level where it stood in the early 1920s.

The Court would be made free to breathe the rarefied air of having to decide "questions of constitutional construction"[11] only.

Taft not only wanted to redefine the Court, to make it the supreme and sole arbiter of the Constitution—a constitutional tribunal of last resort. He wanted the Court to have unfettered power to make policy under the guise of interpreting the Constitution.

Taft's ambition was to make the Supreme Court into a kind of super-legislature whose acts could not be questioned by lower courts or reversed through the ordinary legislative process.

Shortly after Taft was appointed as Chief Justice, he began a lobbying effort that was unprecedented in scope, but commensurate with the extraordinary powers he was seeking on behalf of the Court.

He lobbied for support from the American Bar Association, within both house of Congress, and among his fellow Supreme Court justices (several of whom were doubtful about the proposal).

He even convinced President Coolidge to call for the reform in his first State of the Union message.

In recognition of Taft's exceptional role in advocating the bill, it became known as the "Judges' Bill" even while it was still making its way through Congress.

Remarkably, there was only one member in all of Congress who understood and objected to what Taft was trying to do: Senator Thomas Walsh of Montana, who also happened to be the tenacious investigator who had unearthed the Teapot Dome scandal.

In his reading of the bill, Walsh saw in it evidence of:

> that truism, half legal and half political, that a good court always seeks to extend its jurisdiction, and that other maxim, wholly political...that the appetite for power grows as it is gratified.[12]

Walsh believed that justice was best served by juries composed of ordinary citizens.

Walsh saw in the bill not only Taft's intent to remove power from state courts and local juries, but also his intent to centralize federal power in the Supreme Court.

Despite his warnings against the bill, Walsh stood alone in voicing his concerns.

This was the Roaring Twenties, after all.

Members of Congress could not be bothered to grasp the details of the bill, much less oppose the bill in the name of republican principles.

At this point in the history of our political process, members of Congress were already well down the road of appealing to voters with glittering generalities that most garnered popular applause.

Studying the obscure details of a judiciary bill was not on any congressman's list of top priorities.

It was already fifteen years since Congress had abdicated its legislative power to the executive, through the delegated lawmaking that's still commonplace today.

The Judges' Bill, in its repudiation of checks and balances, reflected a new philosophy of government that had come to guide lawmaking in Congress.

This was an era when Congress, with unlimited faith in the goodwill of men, would grant power to technocrats without limit, and without restraint.

This was the start of the era we still live in today.

For these reasons, the story of the Judges' Bill is cautionary. It shows Congress declining to exercise any judgement whatsoever in the passage of a constitutional enactment of supreme importance.

It's probably no coincidence that the passage of the Judges' Bill came at the tail end of a period that saw near universal adoption of congressional direct primaries.

Since the conditions that eased the passage of the Judges' Bill remain in place, it's no wonder that the Act remains in force today—along with its staggering effects.

* * *

Today, we can't make it through a session of the Supreme Court without at least one ruling that radically alters the settled interpretation of the law.

The reason for this constant uprooting of settled expectations can be found in the Court's unlimited latitude to "decide which cases to decide."

The Court's arbitrary discretion over its docket makes the Court an active agent in the policymaking process.

The writ of certiorari gives the Court the ability to focus on particular issues and controversies, while excluding other issues from its docket, *which amounts to a power of selective enforcement.*

This, in turn, gives the Court the power to engage in a boundless and unrestrained interpretation of the meaning of the Constitution.

The certiorari power, in short, makes the will of a few Supreme Court justices the law of the land.

Unrestricted by institutional restraints, the justices are confined only by the shape-shifting, results-driven legal doctrines that are supposed to guide their efforts.

The writ of certiorari also gives the Court a practically unlimited power to invade the rightful domain of state and local governments.

Thus the modern Supreme Court usurps power from the people while claiming to be their protector, and subverts self-government under the guise of upholding the Constitution.

* * *

Although we're still dealing with the effects of the Judges' Bill today, it only took about six months for the consequences of the Bill to become apparent.

In *Gitlow v. New York*,[13] the Supreme Court used the First Amendment of the Bill of Rights to strike down a state law for the first time in American history.

The ruling struck down a censorship law passed by the New York State legislature.

The *Gitlow* ruling thus established the Incorporation Doctrine, under which the Court has since held most provisions of the federal Bill of Rights applicable to the states.

The Court's continually expanding jurisdiction under the Incorporation Doctrine has greatly increased the role of the Court in policing the constitutionality of state law.

It's worth noting that the framers of the Bill of Rights wrote the First Amendment explicitly so it would *not* apply to state law. Also at that time, the Senate rejected a proposed article, similar to the First Amendment, which began with the words "No *state* shall…"[14]

The Senate did not want to give federal courts the authority—or even the pretense of authority—to encroach upon the states the way the federal courts have, through the Incorporation Doctrine.

Through the Incorporation Doctrine, the Court now has unlimited power to reach into *any* state, overturn *any* law, and in so doing issue a ruling that cannot be reversed by means short of constitutional amendment.

It is a mighty power the Court exercises under the Incorporation Doctrine, and it is a power that is not always exercised with the caution it deserves.

In its boundless zeal to expand its own power, and to bring every question of policy under its all-seeing eye, the Court routinely overreaches its proper authority.

In the final analysis—no matter how much the Court may try to dictate policy through constitutional interpretation—the Court cannot do more than paint in broad strokes and impose one-size-fits-all solutions.

The Court cannot hold public hearings, deliberate on matters of detail, or reach consensus in the way that a legislature can (no matter how imperfect the legislative process may be).

The Court is so far removed from most problems that it deals with today, that it must confine itself to generalities—generalities which do not apply to the circumstances of each and every state and locality.

To the extent the Court has insisted on imposing uniform legal norms, it has eroded the ability of states to compete as "laboratories of democracy."[15]

This imposition of uniformity is also eroding civil and religious liberty in the United States.

The Court's fatal conceit is that nine justices sitting in a chamber in a distant capital know what is best for the people, better than the people know themselves.

But what is truly disturbing about these trends boils down to a simple question.

What happens when the Court makes a *mistake*, under the guise of interpreting the Constitution, and the people have no way to reverse the *mistake*?

Amidst so many rulings that divide our country today, it's possible that the Court may one day issue a ruling which unsettles the very foundations of our Republic.

For all we know, the Court may have already done so, and we just have yet to fully realize the consequences.

In 1857, the Supreme Court decided the *Dred Scott Case* after the controversy had been working its way through the courts for over a decade. The question in the case—whether black slaves were made free by residing in a free state—would decide the fate of slavery throughout the Union.

Chief Justice Roger Taney had no desire to deal with the issue of slavery in a small way, but sought instead to settle the issue "once and for all"—by judicial fiat.

The ruling went so far beyond the meager facts of the case, or any legal issues directly implicated by those facts, that by the time Taney's 54-page ruling was over, he'd struck down an act of Congress that Congress itself had already repealed, he'd overridden the will of the people in more than a dozen states, and he'd declared slavery to be the perpetual law of the land.

What happened next is well known: because the ruling stripped Congress of any power to render a different decision, the ruling so divided the country that it led to civil war.

Today, the power of the Supreme Court makes it far more disruptive, but still no less prone to error, than anyone could've imagined during Roger Taney's long tenure as Chief Justice.

* * *

Today, in its highbrow radicalism, the Court routinely mangles or sets aside laws duly and painstakingly passed through the state or congressional legislative process.

Often, the Court offers no standard in place of the rule it strikes down. Often, the Court offers no hint as to what may be acceptable to its all-seeing, infinite wisdom.

In this manner, the Court undermines the ability of state legislatures, and Congress, to reach important settlements through the legislative process.

This speaks not only to the danger of *entrusting* the Court with too much power, but also to the danger of *allowing* the Court to usurp power from lawmakers.

Hamilton observed in *Federalist* no. 78 that the judiciary possesses "neither FORCE nor WILL, but merely judgment."[16] But the Court has become so powerful that this proverb is no longer true.

Through a subtle accretion of power, the modern Supreme Court exercises authority not only through passive judgment, but also through willful policymaking.

Look at everything the Court does today when it renders a landmark ruling; the Court is so *willful* that it's a completely arbitrary process from beginning to end.

There's so little restraint on the justices that the Court usurps power nearly every time it issues a ruling.

In the final analysis, if we're to curb what constitutional scholar Raoul Berger called "government by judiciary,"[17] we have to stop thinking of judicial activism as a *judicial philosophy*.

We need to look instead at the *lack of institutional restraints* which afford so much latitude to the judges in the first place.

We must begin again to think of the Supreme Court as a creature of the acts of Congress that ordain and establish its jurisdiction and power.

We should not forget that the Constitution gives Congress the power to regulate the appellate jurisdiction of the Supreme Court.

While limiting the Court's appellate jurisdiction would not be without controversy, it would practically bar the Court from intervening in questions better left to state and local self-government.

This action could be undertaken either by repealing statutes like the Judiciary Act of 1925, or by passing new legislation to specifically exclude certain classes of cases from the Court's appellate jurisdiction.

But we also must bear in mind that the centralization of the judiciary is but a reflection of the overall centralization of our political system—and that the overall centralization was wrought by the direct primary.

And so we probably will not curb the excessive federal intervention in our local affairs, until we first restore our power of self-government, through the indirect primary.

There are people who deny that Congress has the power to alter judiciary acts of its own creation.[18]

But upon that power of Congress may rest the salvation of our Republic.

14

The Triumph of Ideological Polarization

The two-party system lies at the heart of our uniquely American system of self-government.

Yet more Americans are disenchanted with the two-party system than ever before in our history.

As the major parties work harder each election cycle to alienate an ever-larger share of the electorate, many people have simply abandoned the two-party system as a worthwhile mode of political expression.

Today, we tend to overlook what makes our party system good, how it developed, and why it's actually worth preserving.

People forget—or never learned in the first place—that the parties were created to give ordinary people a voice in the political process.

Today, despite the prevailing attitude toward parties, party involvement is still the most effective way for citizens to engage in the process of self-governance.

Yet it's also true that the major parties no longer serve their function; so *few* people are involved today that the parties do *not* represent the views of *most* people.

This is not just unfortunate; it's potentially ruinous.

As people turn away from the major parties, or refuse to get involved, they are, in effect, rejecting the uniquely effective mode of political expression the parties afford.

We cannot hope to restore our republican institutions, much less preserve them, if ordinary people remain as alienated from the party system as they are today.

* * *

The number one myth about American political parties is that the framers of the Constitution did not condone their existence.

This myth is true only in a very narrow sense that ignores what the framers *said* and, more importantly, ignores what they *did*.

What was the ratification of the Constitution, after all, if not a partisan contest of epic proportions, even before political parties in the modern sense had been formed?

When people like John Adams and George Washington condemned party, faction, and the spirit of party, they had in mind a specific set of issues.

As Richard Hofstadter observed in *The Idea of a Party System*:

> Party was associated with painfully deep and unbridgeable differences in national politics, with religious bigotry and clerical animus, with treason and the threat of foreign invasion, with instability and dangers to liberty.[1]

"Faction" was considered the worst possible manifestation of party, and was often associated with tumult, violence, and insurrection.

Thus parties were viewed not as creatures *within* the political system, but as entities which would *fundamentally constitute or subvert* the political order.

Years before the Constitution was formed, John Adams lamented, "There is nothing which I dread so much as a division of the republic into two great parties, *each arranged under its leader.*"[2]

At the Federal Convention, Madison described the varieties of "Sects, Factions, & interests" which exist in any society, among which he listed *"the followers of this political leader or that."*[3]

These observations suggest a truth that is still valid today: candidate-centered factionalism is the most vicious form of political strife that exists in any system.

These factions are not parties in the modern sense. In fact, it's *extremely significant* that the Founding Fathers were so concerned about the dangers of factionalism in the era before modern parties were created.

Modern political parties consist of a permanent, institutionalized party organization that transcends and outlasts particular candidates and political leaders.

Modern political parties could not be more different from the narrow, candidate-centered cliques that overran the political process in the early years of our Republic.

When Washington warned against the "spirit of Party" in his Farewell Address, he had in mind the self-interested factions of his own era: factions that revolved around wealthy patrons and prominent demagogues who cared little about the interests of the country.

When Washington looked upon the "disorders and miseries" of partisan conflict, he foretold that they would "incline the minds of men to seek security and repose in the absolute power of an individual."

But we must accept Washington's warning with an understanding of the institutional context.

Washington's real concern, it may be argued, was the *style* of politics that would prevail if personal factions, centered on candidates, were left unchecked as the dominant mode of political organization.

But in truth, this mode of political organization prevails *in default of* party organization.

The candidate-centered mode of political organization is dominant today—as it was in the early years—but only because the direct primary has disemboweled the parties.

* * *

As American political institutions matured, and as parties became established in the political landscape, American politicians began to develop an appreciation of the need for political parties.

This realization allowed legitimate party opposition to take root.

Legitimate party opposition soon came to be recognized as a crucial check on political power—a check tantamount to the checks within the Constitution itself.

Martin Van Buren was the most prominent champion of the new party system. When he retired after decades of involvement in state and national politics, Van Buren would write one of the most important defenses of the American party system ever written.

He viewed political parties as "inseparable from free governments" and professed that "I never could bring myself for party purposes to deprecate their existence. Doubtless...[parties] produce many evils, but not so many as are prevented by [them]."[4]

He went on to observe of parties that, "The disposition to abuse power, so deeply planted in the human heart, can by no other means be more effectually checked."[5]

Legitimate party opposition fostered through a party system does more than just prevent the abuse of power. Parties also serve to vet candidates, concentrate votes, and stabilize the electoral process.

Parties may also serve to moderate political discourse and give citizens a greater voice in the process, provided the parties are governed under sound rules.

* * *

Once the vital constitutional role of the party system is accepted, the question then is: what is the optimal number of political parties?

The reason the two-party system is best can be fully appreciated only by considering the only alternatives to the two-party system that are known to have existed.

Under *one-party rule*, there is no legitimate political opposition. The ruling party enjoys full control of the political system, which gives officials unchecked power. This can have a chilling effect on free speech and often leads to the outright suppression of dissent.

Under *multiparty rule*, the ruling coalition may be checked by organized opposition or not, depending on how fragmented the party system becomes. Regardless, the controlling party often lacks the legitimacy of having obtained a majority.

Multiparty rule often yields a fragmented party system that cannot vet candidates or moderate appeals made by candidates.

Because multiparty rule allows extremists to win elected office, the system often leads to demands for censorship, which in turn abridges free speech.

Because both alternatives to the two-party system lead to the repression of free speech, we might say the two-party system is an essential (though relatively unacknowledged) safeguard for free speech.

Once the vital link between the two-party system and free speech is understood, the question then is how to establish and maintain a two-party system.

Although Van Buren assumed permanent, two-party opposition to be ordained by human nature, this assumption was incorrect.

We can see by comparing our political process to many countries around the world that the structure of the party system—i.e., the number, composition, and size of the parties—is *not* ordained by nature.

Many people casually assume that we congregate into two parties—no more and no fewer—due to some intrinsic genius in the American people.

But this is simply not true.

Even within the two major parties in the United States, we can observe a high degree of nuance among the factions within each party, and in the way each faction prioritizes and seeks to address issues.

What prevents the major parties from dissolving into their component factions, even to the point of disintegrating into single-issue parties?

In reality, the American two-party system is the product of our winner-take-all electoral process, which forces parties and candidates to build majority coalitions in order to win elections.[6]

Similarly, the multiparty rule in other countries is the product of proportional voting, which allows parties and candidates to win elections through narrower appeals.

We might further note that in the early years of our Republic, when many states chose all members of their congressional delegation in a single, statewide election, this process fostered one-party rule at the national level.[7]

The point is simply this: the number of viable political parties is determined by the electoral structure, not just in other countries but in the United States as well.

By recognizing the institutional basis of the party system—rather than its supposed social origins—we can see the conditions needed to preserve our system.

And it's worth repeating: the winner-take-all structure is needed not only to preserve the two-party system, but also to protect free speech—which is really the ultimate purpose of the two-party system.

Two specific practices have allowed the two-party system to flourish in the United States.

These practices have nothing to do with the fund-raising networks, donor habits, brand identification, or other "sociological causes" which are typically understood to form the basis of our two-party system.

Generally speaking, the two-party system arose out of our single-member, winner-take-all electoral process.

"Single-member" means that only one elected official is chosen from a given district or ballot position.

"Winner-take-all" means the plurality or majority victor wins the election outright. No seats are given to any minority party on the basis of a proportional vote.

We can compare this—our present system—with the *multi-member*, winner-take-all system of our early

Republic, in which entire congressional delegations were elected by statewide majority vote.[8]

We can also compare our present system with the *multi-member proportional* systems of other countries, which yield *multiparty* rule.

There are two key elements that form the basis of our winner-take-all election system in the United States.

The first element is single-member legislative districts. Single-member districts, by their very nature, require candidates to win a plurality or a majority in order to win election.

The second element of our winner-take-all election system is the statewide, winner-take-all elections that we use to appoint presidential electors to the Electoral College. The statewide elections used in the Electoral College make each state a kind of "single-member district" in the presidential electoral vote.

The combined effect of these winner-take-all systems makes it very difficult for any third party movement, no matter how well organized, to gain much traction in our political process.

But the other effect of our winner-take-all system is often overlooked, especially during fits of hubris within the majority party.

When pundits and operatives begin to speak of the prospects of a "permanent majority"[9] party, you know the reigning majority is about to suffer a major loss at the polls.

Under our present single-member, winner-take-all electoral system, there is not, and *never can be*, a permanent majority party in the United States.

CARL JARVIS

We *could* have a permanent majority, but only by first making radical changes to the structure of our electoral process.

* * *

Given the importance of the two-party system as a check against political power, and as a safeguard for free speech, we should regard with caution any effort to alter or abolish the institutional basis of that system.

More specifically, given the role of the Electoral College and single-member districts in preserving the two-party system, we should view with extreme caution any proposal to alter those institutions.

With respect to electoral reform, there seem to be two types of reform advocates: those who understand what they propose, but don't admit the consequences; and those for whom the best course would be to learn what they think they already know.

Today, there are those who would abolish the Electoral College to bring an end to the two-party system. But there are many more people who would abolish the Electoral College because they do not understand the wide-ranging consequences of what they propose.

Abolishing the Electoral College would admit demagogues into the presidential election process to a degree that's unimaginable, even today.

Similarly, there are those who say that we should replace our single-member legislative districts with proportional legislative representation.

What these people fail to admit—or fail to realize—is that abolishing winner-take-all elections would not just dissolve our two-party system.

The dissolution of our two-party system would paralyze our political process, and perhaps even bring an end to our republican form of government.

* * *

The danger of dissolving the two-party system may seem unreal, especially given the extreme dysfunction of the two major political parties today.

So we need to begin by acknowledging the valid concerns of those who criticize the monopoly control the major parties have over our political process.

We need to acknowledge that "the tyranny of the two-party system,"[10] of which the critics speak, is real.

The question then becomes what to do about it.

Today, our two-party system has become so polarized that the major parties no longer represent the views of most Americans, views that are rooted in experience and common sense rather than political ideology.

Polarization is also eroding the ability of our political leaders to address the problems we face, and it's destroying our ability to govern ourselves as a people.

But polarization is not inherent to the two-party system.

The American two-party system coalesced during the 1830s; but the radicalization of the two-party system began only in the twentieth century.

How can we explain this shift?

The radicalization of the major parties seems to have resulted from changes made to American election laws.

Up until the 1890s, the method of voting was by party ticket. Party tickets were printed and distributed by the parties and voters used the tickets to vote on Election Day, by depositing the party tickets into the ballot box.

Party tickets were essential to the conduct of elections, not unlike the ballots we use today.

The problem with the party ticket was that the parties could mark the ballots with distinct colors and other insignia to monitor the ballots cast by voters.

The states could have eliminated the problem by regulating the appearance of the party tickets.

Instead, states began to pass official ballot laws that served to eliminate the party tickets altogether.

First introduced in 1888, official ballot laws were adopted throughout the United States by 1896.[11]

With the adoption of official ballot laws, the appearance of the ballot—and especially the order of candidates and parties on the ballot—came under the control and administration of the state.

Practically overnight, third party movements faced ballot access requirements they had not had to contend with just a few years prior.

Ballot access aside, now third parties also had to contend with the arrangement of the ballot, which gave top billing to the major parties

It would be hard to overstate the impact of the official ballot in changing the character of the political parties.

The foremost effect of the official ballot was to create barriers to entry against third party movements.

Before the official ballot, parties had been voluntary private associations whose success depended entirely on their viability in the political marketplace.

After the adoption of the official ballot, the major parties became more like "quasi-public regulated utilities."[12] No longer *independent* of the state, the major parties began to morph into *appendages* of the state.

This change in the character of the parties had many subtle yet far-reaching effects on the two-party system.

Just a few years after the official ballot was adopted in all fifty states, third parties—which had become less viable—nearly vanished from the political landscape.

In retrospect, the 1892 election marked the high tide of third party movements in the United States.

In the presidential election that year, the Populist Party won 8.5% of the popular vote along with twenty-two electoral votes.[13]

This would be the last election in which a splinter movement, organized as a third party on a national basis, would achieve such a degree of electoral success.

By the 1896 election, the Populist Party had become a mere label, and ceased to exist independent from the Democratic Party organization.

The trend evident in presidential politics could be observed in Congress as well.

In 1897, there were around forty third-party members of Congress.[14] By 1903, there were none.[15]

The reason for this rapid disappearance of third party candidates from elected office in the United States may seem like a mystery. But it was undoubtedly the effect of official ballot laws and the obstacles they posed to third party movements.

Before the official ballot came into existence, there remained the possibility that a third party might gain enough traction to overtake and unseat one of the two major parties.

After the official ballot became widely adopted, however, it made more sense for a candidate to contend *within* a major party, than for a candidate to try to contend from *without*.

Conflicts that had formerly played out *between parties* on Election Day would now take place *among candidates* in the nominating process.

Thus the entire process shifted from competition *between parties* to competition *between candidates*.

This shift was certainly among the major causes of direct primary reform. The direct primary seemed to level the playing field between candidates, as it allowed all candidates to compete openly for the prize of appearing on the ballot on Election Day.

Direct primaries also had a flip side. By reducing the parties to mere labels that we assign to independent candidates, direct primary nomination made the parties indistinguishable on matters of principle.

This lack of a meaningful distinction between the parties was a real problem under the direct primary system, even in its early days.

As one critic of the system, Simon Adler, observed:

> there is no method under [the direct primary system] by which a party can rid itself of members who merely take its name and abandon its doctrine.[16]

So it remains today.

Even worse than the lack of difference between the major parties is the disturbing similarity they share in common.

Today, both parties engage in a kind of populism and emotionalism that was relegated to the extreme political fringes, prior to the adoption of the direct primary.

* * *

Mainstream political discourse in the United States has become polarized and prone to extremism, over the course of the last one hundred years.

This condition has given rise to the *hope* that a third party movement might one day emerge to displace one or both of the major parties.

But this is a fantasy that is not supported by the logic of our present electoral system.

For any third party to make a meaningful difference would first require the party to defy the institutional basis that makes the two-party system what it is today.

Within the present system, it's doubtful—to say the least—that a third party movement could ever evolve into a major party while remaining true to any principle that it started with.

But let's even suppose the rise of a third party willing to stand for nothing, and to serve as a mere label, in a headlong effort to unseat one of the major parties. The last time a third party overtook a major party was when the Republicans supplanted the Whigs *in the 1850s.*

The rise of the Republican Party demonstrated the flexibility of the "original" two-party system. But the flexibility of the original system went the way of the party ticket, which is to say: it no longer exists.

Whether we like it or not, the "quasi-public regulated" character of the major parties leads to two conclusions.

First, working within one of the major political parties is vastly more effective than trying to influence the political process from the outside, through a third party.

Second, improving the laws that regulate the major parties would be the most lasting and effective way to restore self-government in the United States.

Unfortunately, the state laws that regulate the parties are overwhelmingly ignored.

Today, we don't see many proposals to improve the party system. Instead, we see proposals that would have the effect of abolishing our two-party system.

Thomas Mann and Norman Ornstein, for example, commend proportional representation as a possible remedy for the ills of our present two-party system. They say:

> Some form of [proportional representation] would reduce the impact of gerrymandering, increase turnout, better represent minority interests...and *encourage depolarization of the current party system.*[17]

Robert Richie and Steven Hill have similarly asserted:

> *governance is more likely to take place at the center of the political spectrum with [proportional representation],* since the electorate is fully represented and voters are able to express a wider range of preferences.[18]

Many people would like to be able to elect "just a moderate party," a party that would govern from the center and pursue common sense policies.

These proposals for proportional representation clearly speak to that desire.

But these proposals also suggest a looming danger.

The danger is that we've become so disillusioned by the polarization and dysfunction of the major parties that we're increasingly receptive to radical nostrums.

Proposals that would dissolve our two-party system are praised, often without any thought at all as to the real consequences.

Just because a proposal would dissolve the two-party system does not mean it would substitute something better in its place.

The promise of proportional representation, in particular, is extremely deceptive, to say the least.

There are two things every American should know before proportional representation is ever seriously considered as a way to get rid of our two-party system in the United States.

First, proportional representation was the system that allowed the rise of Adolf Hitler in Germany and Benito Mussolini in Italy during the 1930s.[19]

Second, proportional representation promoted the election of extremists, even in *cities* where it was adopted in the United States during the 1930s and afterward.

Let's take a look each of these historical facts in greater detail.

Although advocates of proportional representation dismiss the rise of Hitler and Mussolini as exceptions, and blame economic conditions for the rise of fascism in Germany and Italy, the facts do not support their claim.

During the 1930s, every country in the world fell into economic depression. Three countries in particular—the United States, Great Britain, and France—defied the slide into extremism that occurred elsewhere. These countries remained stable because each had a two-party system that prevented extremists from being elected to office in large numbers.[20]

While advocates of proportional representation claim the system would not foster political extremism in the United States, again the facts do not support their claim.

During the 1930s, when proportional representation was adopted in New York City, it allowed communists and other radicals (under a variety of party labels) to be elected to the city council in numbers that exceeded their statistical strength in the electorate.[21]

In other words, proportional representation actually *magnified* the influence of political extremists.

While it's true that proportional representation would fulfill the dream of dissolving our two-party system, it would do so in a manner that would destroy our entire political system.

* * *

While proportional representation is touted as a sure *remedy* for the ills of our two-party system, the real *cause* of the polarization and extremism we see today is none other than the *direct primary system itself.*

The reality of the direct primary system is this: less than a third of eligible voters vote in the primaries.

Among those who do vote, few possess complete information about every candidate in every race. This creates confusion in how voters perceive candidates.

The confusion gives candidates every incentive to appeal to primary voters with the most polarizing, emotional, hot button issue they can identify.

Incidentally, the logic of the process creates further disgust toward the political system when candidates later "flip flop" on issues, after winning the primary.

The emotional appeals elicited by the direct primary are inherent to the system. This is not a problem with the voters who show up to the polls or with the candidates who run for office. *The problem is in the system itself.*

Nor do these effects pertain only to one party, as some like to claim; *the effects of the direct primary system are felt—and reflected—by* both *major parties.*

The direct primary is the main reason for the erosion of the center, and gravitation toward extremes, that can be seen in American politics over the past century.

Thus the way to restore the center is *not* by proportional representation, but by abolishing the direct primary and switching the system to an indirect basis.

The indirect primary would not only curb political extremism. It would also reduce the apathy, disgust, and cynicism that taint the general perception of politics today.

The indirect primary would draw ordinary citizens into the process and reduce the sense of alienation that is crippling our country today.

Many people *feel* the direct primary gives them a voice, but *feel* is the operative word.

In reality, the direct primary process is *entirely controlled* by outrageous sums of money.

With elections awash in moneyed influence today, it's no wonder the people have lost control over the direction of government.

The indirect primary would restore the influence of ordinary people because it would give them an effective voice in the selection of candidates.

It would empower the people to govern themselves once again.

Unfortunately, even after so much experience with the direct primary, many still view the effects of the direct primary as *incidental*—and not as *inherent* to the system.

This fosters the illusion that we can somehow *keep* the direct primary but *manage* its less desirable effects.

Charles Merriam, a major advocate of direct primary reform during the Progressive Era, expressed disappointment in 1928 at "the failure of the voter to exercise his hard-won franchise"[22] in the primaries.

Today, the effect of low voter turnout can be seen in the hyper-emotional appeals some candidates use to turnout their supporters on Primary Day.

Candidates must appeal to voters at a visceral level—not only to *win votes*, but also to *ensure their supporters shows up at the polls in the first place.*

Because of this dynamic, candidates win by appealing to the deeper—and sometimes darker—recesses of the human psyche.

This is why boring but increasingly urgent issues like budget defects are never really discussed—much less addressed—other than the obligatory lip service.

The way to fix the problem is not to get *more* voters—or *more intelligent* voters—to show up at the polls.

The way to fix the problem is to change the way the *process* works.

Indirect primaries would end candidates' incentive to engage in demagoguery, because candidates' names would not appear on the primary ballot.

Instead, voters would be choosing a delegate to select the candidate on their behalf.

The *delegate candidate* would not use the kind of demagogic appeals that *candidates* do, because the delegate would not have the prospect of attaining the power necessary to fulfill specific campaign promises.

Delegate candidates would find it useful only to express the beliefs, principles, and criteria that would guide them in selecting a *candidate* at the convention.

Thus the indirect primary would curb—and perhaps even *end*—the kind of poll-driven, flavor-of-the-moment issues that dominate our politics today.

Using the indirect primary to mediate candidate selection would eliminate the most dangerous effect of the direct primary, which is the type of appeal it elicits from successful candidates.

In 1928, two decades after publishing his initial treatise on primary elections, even Merriam admitted his frustration at "the defeat of conspicuously desirable candidates by rogues and demagogues as the result of [the effects of the direct primary]."[23]

* * *

The real danger of ideological polarization is not the endless bickering, the broken promises, or even the bizarre policies we see in American politics today.

The real danger of polarization is the gathering crisis of confidence it is visiting upon our political institutions.

Today, people increasingly view our Constitution as fatally flawed.

This disillusionment does not stem from any fault in the Constitution itself. It is entirely due to the broken political process that surrounds the Constitution.

Today, people are increasingly persuaded that we need radical solutions to the crisis we face.

And given current trends, it's only a matter of time before we enact a cure, like proportional representation, that ends up being far worse than the disease.

Today, political dysfunction is precipitating a loss of faith in our institutions, which is giving way to something far more dangerous.

The real peril we presently face is that we've become so distracted by irrelevant issues that most people don't see what's happening to our system.

Our country is on the verge of succumbing to tyranny, which may take the form of legislative mob rule or executive dictatorship, and we've lost faith in the very Constitution which stands between us and that fate.

By its very nature, ideological polarization induces political leaders to pander to narrow constituencies rather than act with the good of the country in mind.

Worse yet, ideological polarization induces ordinary people to favor radical proposals that would lead us to abandon the institutions that made our country great.

Today, if ideological polarization is making America ungovernable, it's worth pondering the one aspect of our system that's causing all the trouble.

Rather than abandoning our Constitution, or giving up on our two-party system, we'd be far better off if we addressed the problem at its root.

Like so many other problems that are destroying our capacity for self-government, the polarization of American politics was born of the direct primary.

The way to restore self-government in America—along with political sanity—is to restore the *indirect* primary.

PART IV

Vision:
Government of, by, and for the People Restored

A free people cannot govern themselves without intermediary institutions to facilitate self-government.

Political parties are—and always have been—the *chief* intermediary institutions through which free people govern their own affairs.

This is true not only of the modern United States; it's true of *any* free country in the world today; and also it's true of *every* free country that's ever existed.

Parties serve as a check against political incumbents— and thus as a restraint against government power.

Political parties give the people a voice through a mode of influence that is independent of elected officials.

Political parties are lasting institutions, equipped to oversee government on a continual basis.

But political parties cannot serve their basic purpose unless ordinary citizens take part in *party governance*.

Under our political system, *party governance* is virtually identical to *self-governance*, so intertwined are the parties with the people's ability to govern themselves.

Political parties are so important that even a dysfunctional party system gives ordinary people far more influence than they would have in a purely candidate-centered political process.

Candidate-centered campaign organizations are inherently ad hoc, temporary, and subject to the whims of the candidate or elected official.

A well-organized party system, on the other hand, not only mirrors the structure of constitutional government, with its vertical and horizontal separation of powers.

A well-organized party system also strengthens that structure, and turns out of office any elected official that would seek to undermine the form of the Constitution.

For all the advantages of political parties, they *can't work* unless ordinary people participate in the *business* of party governance.

For all the advantages of political parties, they *won't work* unless the party system is vested with *proper intermediary powers* and constituted as a *meaningful avenue of political participation*.

Intermediary institutions like parties are sometimes said to buffer the people *away* from government.

But nothing could be further from the truth.

The truth is that we cannot have self-government in the United States—which I take to mean a condition of *government of, by, and for the people*—unless the people would first govern themselves through *party governance*.

15

The Citizen's Role in Self-Government

The great question of our day is whether the American people—or really any people possessed of the frailties of human nature—are truly capable of self-government.

The framers of our Constitution thought so; and, despite their doubts, they answered the question in the affirmative.

Today, we stand at a point in history *unlike* any before it, but also *not unlike* the challenging times and crises navigated by our forefathers.

It's interesting that we've grown so complacent today that people take for granted a Constitution formed under such perils and at such great personal sacrifice, by a group of people who had so little to guide them in such an unprecedented enterprise.

It's easy to forget that the Constitution was born into a benighted world of kings and despots; and that even the framers themselves were not sure whether it would work.

It's also easy to forget that they created the Constitution so that we wouldn't need a king or a ruler.

They wanted to empower the people to govern themselves in a manner that was unprecedented in that day and age.

Out of the experiment in self-government they began sprung the mightiest nation the world has ever known.

Given the heights to which we've ascended, it's easy to take the system that made it possible for granted.

Yet we each have a role—and a responsibility—not only to preserve our form of government, but also to make it work on a day to day basis.

* * *

Today people are losing faith in our political system because they're losing confidence in the political leaders that have failed them again and again.

Yet the answer to the crisis we face is not to lose faith in the system, but rather to restore the system and make it worthy of our faith once again.

Political leaders will inevitably disappoint us, but it's not the attitude of a self-governing people to concern themselves with the failings of political leaders.

Instead, we must carefully and selectively invest our time and energy in the activities that most directly support the condition of self-government.

Self-government requires citizens not to be *merely* engaged—but to be *intelligently* engaged—in the process of self-governance.

Today, as always, many avenues of civic and political involvement are available. There are opportunities at the local, state, and national level, and none of these should be overlooked.

But given all of the opportunities, where does a person begin?

You *may* find that the single most effective way for you to participate in the process of self-government would be as a precinct chairman in your local party.

Precinct chairmen are the local party officials who represent their neighborhoods in local county parties throughout the United States.

Precinct chairmen influence all types of party business as voting members of the county executive committees.

Even more importantly, precinct chairmen gain first-hand experience in how our political process works that most people don't have.

To gain a similar appreciation, but with less time commitment than precinct chairs incur, also consider serving as a county or state convention delegate.[1]

The great thing about these party offices is that they're within the reach of just about anyone who would take the initiative to pursue them.

In many states, you can become a precinct chair simply by registering with the local county clerk to appear on the primary ballot.

You may be opposed or unopposed in the primary. If unopposed, you become the precinct chair by default.

Even if you are opposed in the primary, the most effort that's required is to canvass the primary voters in your own neighborhood.

In many states, becoming a convention delegate is even easier. Research the delegate selection process, show up at the precinct caucus, and have your name placed on the delegate list for the upcoming convention.

Given the influence and "insider status" that precinct chairmen and convention delegates have, it's no wonder these positions are among the most jealously guarded in our political system.

* * *

Billions of dollars are spent on political advertising each election cycle, yet few people realize how easy it is to become a convention delegate—and fewer still will have even *heard of* the position of precinct chairman.

That these positions are unadvertised—and unknown to most people—speaks volumes about our present crisis of self-governance in the United States.

In many cases, ordinary people are not recruited to these positions because that would upset the status quo preferred by those who control each party.

The situation with precinct chairmanships is especially illuminating.

In the state of New York, unless you've been invited, you can forget about being appointed as a precinct chair before the next primary election.

They don't make it easy to file and run for the position either. In New York, it's difficult even to find out what precinct you reside in, what its exact boundaries are, and whether there's a vacancy in the precinct chair position.

In certain areas of Texas, the precinct chairmanships are so tightly controlled that it may be senseless for you to seek an appointment before the next primary election.

At least Texas, unlike New York, makes it's easy to file and run for the position in the primary.

Remarkably, in these states, there's a general policy of exclusion in appointing precinct chairs, even in counties where half the precinct chairmanships are vacant; and even in counties where the executive committee can't meet the legally required quorum to do business.

These exclusionary policies are entirely a symptom of the top-down, centralized control of the political parties enabled by the direct primary.

This kind of top-down control is inevitable under a system in which even local party leaders are chosen by direct primary election in many states.

The way to counter the top-down, exclusionary control of the parties would be to reorganize the party system around the indirect primary.

The indirect primary would empower grassroots activists with greater influence in the party system—and thus in the political process overall.

The indirect primary would allow citizens not only to *pass resolutions* at the conventions—resolutions that candidates disregard under the present system—but it would also allow citizens to *select candidates* to carry out those resolutions.

In other words, *ordinary citizens* would select candidates—as opposed to the *moneyed influence* that prevails in the candidate selection process today.

The ability to actually influence *important decisions* would act as an incentive for more people to get involved at the grassroots level of the political parties.

Remarkably, the shift from direct to indirect primaries would not require an act of Congress, a ruling by the Supreme Court, or a constitutional amendment.

The shift to the indirect primary would be brought about by modifying state party rules in some cases; by changing state law in others; and by changing state and national party rules in the case of the presidential nominating process.[2]

Even more remarkably, it would take only a small group of people to carry out the change: far fewer than the number who fought in the American Revolution; and yet the effect would be no less momentous.

With the experience in party governance you gain as a precinct chairman or convention delegate, you may have the chance to help play a role in this transformation.

* * *

In a day and age when people want to know what can be done to save our country—some advocate a constitutional convention or amendments, while others press for outright nullification of federal acts—the indirect primary would be a uniquely effective way to combat the creeping tyranny of the central government.

At the same time, the prolonged presidential races of recent years suggest that the presidential nominating process would be especially fertile ground on which to demonstrate the effects of the indirect primary.

The 2008 Democratic race and the 2012 Republican race were so drawn out that there was a long period of uncertainty as to the final outcome.

In both cases, the prolonged races prompted media speculation that a "brokered convention" might select the final nominee.

In reality, a brokered convention was never in the cards, in either case, for the simple reason that most states use direct primaries to send delegates to the national conventions.

Direct primaries require a candidate preference vote.

And the binding nature of the candidate preference vote, conducted by so many states, practically precludes a brokered convention.

Even states that don't hold actual direct primaries often hold straw polls, which have the same effect.

While straw polls do not *formally* bind delegates, their effect on the prospects for a brokered convention is virtually the same, as if a direct primary had been held.

To have a true brokered convention, you would need to have a large number of delegates who were not pledged or committed to any candidate in advance.

Despite widespread media speculation to the contrary, let the record show that we did not have a brokered convention in 2008, or in 2012.

Yet there is one major implication of the dynamics of both races that is worth dwelling on.

If the recent pattern of prolonged open seat races for the presidency holds, then we're assured not one, but two, long and closely fought presidential nominating races in 2016; and at least one more, again, in 2020.

From the standpoint of the transformative potential of the indirect primary, the implications of this fact are staggering.

Today, conventional wisdom holds that a state must set its primary date as early in the schedule as possible, in order to maximize its influence over the presidential nominating decision of both parties.

While losing in the early states can prematurely end a campaign, winning in an early state like Iowa or New Hampshire can propel a candidate to the nomination.[3]

The results in the early states affect the results in the later states, because nearly every state in the process uses candidate preference voting.

This gives early states an influence that is totally out of proportion to the number of delegates they send to the national conventions.

Yet the influence of the early states hinges on the *assumption* that candidate preference voting will be used in most—if not all—of the presidential primaries held.

But what if a few states—or one large state—elected only convention delegates, refused to hold a candidate preference primary, and *declined to record or publicize any candidate preference vote or straw poll* in the reporting of its presidential primary results?

Under the closely fought dynamics of recent races, Iowa and New Hampshire would indeed have the "first word," with their pledged delegates.

But several small states—or a large state like Texas—could have the "last word," if they sent uncommitted delegates to the convention rather than delegates pledged to a particular candidate.

Under the tightly contested dynamics of recent races, the uncommitted delegates would hold the balance of power at the convention, and would potentially decide the outcome of the race.

But here's a critical detail that's worth repeating: for a scenario like this to unfold, it would be essential for uncommitted delegates to be selected without any expression of candidate preference *whatsoever*: that is, no candidates' names on the primary ballot, no straw polls, and preferably no exit polling by the media.

A *true* indirect primary—even in just a few critical states—would allow *duly elected delegates* to exercise judgment and discretion at the national convention.[4]

Such a change would not only restore the influence of *ordinary citizens* in the selection of presidential candidates through the national convention system.

With the realization that such change is possible—and with the demonstrated proof of its effect—it would quite possibly transform our entire political system from top to bottom.

* * *

If the indirect primary would reorder power among the states, it could be even more advantageously disruptive in the contest between the parties.

Conventional wisdom holds that presidential hopefuls must begin raising money years in advance, organize in states like Iowa and New Hampshire years in advance, and declare their candidacy years in advance.

None of this offers any guarantee of the nomination, but only the *chance to viably compete* for it.

But what if this process were turned on its head?

While it is admittedly more speculative than the "state scenario," what would happen if one of the major parties changed its rules to forbid all state parties from sending pledged delegates to its national convention?

In effect, this would force the associated state parties to hold delegate selection primaries only, with no candidate preference expressed or reported.

Under such conditions, initiative would be wrested from the candidates.

The party could hold its nominating process in suspense until the assembling of its national convention, conserving its energy and marshaling its resources.

The convention would then be free to select the most qualified and suitable candidate, rather than the candidate most adept at garnering popular applause.

At the same time, the *other* party would be wading through the quagmire of the candidate preference primary process. As the field of candidates narrowed, the contest would become even more bitter and contentious.

By the time this *other* party selected its nominee, the party would be exhausted, demoralized, and broke. Without so much as pausing to mend its internal lacerations, the party would turn toward Election Day to face a unified juggernaut flush with cash.

* * *

The dynamics of the "state" and "party" scenarios suggest that if a few states, or one party, were to adopt the indirect primary, this would force other participants to do so as well, in order to remain viable.

Such a punctuated switch may *seem* unlikely, but rapid changes to the presidential nominating process have occurred on several previous occasions.

Two of those occasions, in particular, yielded a transformation of our entire political system.

The first transformation occurred in 1828. This was the election that made Andrew Jackson president. Prior to his election, sons were inheriting offices from their fathers, the elite controlled the economy through the machinery of a central bank, and the country had what amounted to a system of one-party rule.

During his tenure, Jackson renewed rotation in office, ended the Second Bank of the United States, and rejuvenated the party system.

In doing so, he unleashed the power of the American spirit and spurred an entrepreneurial revolution that lasted for nearly one hundred years.

Given the dramatic change that took place after his election, it's remarkable that Jackson would not have been elected without the party convention system that brought him to power.

The second major transformation of the presidential nominating process began in 1912.

This was the election that made Woodrow Wilson President and brought to power a regime that was in every way a counter-revolution against Jackson's legacy.

Prior to Wilson's presidency, the tradition of government of, by, and for the people, forged during the Jacksonian Period, was still largely intact.

During Wilson's tenure, he thoroughly eradicated most aspects of our political system that had previously shielded the people from government power.

Wilson erected a bureaucracy over and above the people which grows increasingly oppressive by the year.

He established a central bank that continues to rob the people of their savings and livelihoods.

He engineered a realignment of the party system that made the parties indistinguishable from one another; and he implanted a kind of elite rule not seen in America since the very early years of our Republic.

Wilson's presidency marked the start of an era that has witnessed staggering growth in government alongside the rise of unchecked presidential power.

In accomplishing all of this, Wilson's supreme coup was to overturn the Constitution in the space of years, in ways most people still do not even recognize.

Just as Jackson brought the common people to power, Wilson brought the mandarins, the intellectuals, and the self-anointed guardians with him to office.

This tiny elite has remained in power ever since, and its members share a common fatal conceit. They think they know better than you how you should live your life.

Just as with Jackson, so with Wilson: Wilson would not have been elected without the changes that were made to the presidential nominating process.

Wilson well understood the nature of the change that was underway. In fact, he was one of the main academic proponents of the direct primary system.

When the 1912 Democratic Convention deadlocked, Wilson was presented as the man who would rise above politics and transcend the fray: a patriot king possessed of all-seeing wisdom.

Wilson's messianic bent would become a model for later presidents, who mimicked his rhetoric and became similarly deluded by the powers of the office.

Today, as we find our liberties and fortunes ruined by the philosopher-kings that Wilson brought to power, the people clamor ever more loudly for a political redeemer.

Alas, our country cannot be saved by the work of any single person. It will be saved only by the invisible hand of a nominating process built to conform to the everlasting principles of our Constitution.

* * *

Anyone who doubts the transformative power of the nominating process should study with care these two singularly important presidential elections.

These elections demonstrate just how nontrivial the nominating process is, because they demonstrate the total extent to which the mode of nomination dictates conditions throughout our political system.

Presidential history offers dramatic proof of the power of the nominating process; but the effects of the mode of nomination range far beyond the presidency.

It's no exaggeration to say that changing the mode of nomination has transformed our country twice before.

A similar change can—and would—do so again.

The secret of the indirect primary lies in its ability to empower ordinary citizens with a meaningful voice in the political process.

The question isn't whether the change back to the indirect primary would have the necessary effect. The question is whether we have the courage and will to restore the indirect primary.

The story of the mode of nomination may seem like an obscure footnote in the history of our great country.

And indirect primary reform may seem far removed from the immense crisis we presently face.

But the struggle over the mode of nomination marks the battlefield where America will be won or lost.

For the sake of millions yet unborn, let us have the courage to pursue the fight.

CONCLUSION

Are We Rome?

Bound by tribal loyalties, unrestrained by checks and balances, and fueled by demagogic appeals, our politics today are a portrait of what James Madison must have imagined when he spoke of "the mischiefs of faction."

In the haze of petty partisanship, leaderless drift, and endless finger pointing, the spirit of faction that prevails in our politics today has yielded a dangerous concentration of power in the hands of the Few.

Some may find it hard to believe that such a seemingly minor institution as the direct primary could be the cause of so much chaos and dysfunction.

After all, who would have thought that such an obscure change as replacing delegates' names with candidates' names on a primary ballot could yield the disaster that we have before us today?

Only by looking past the *promise* of the direct primary and to its *effects*, can you begin to fathom how corrosive the direct primary is to our republican institutions.

Even after you've trained your eye on the effects of the direct primary, those effects can be hard to see because they so pervade American politics today.

The direct primary is used to select candidates for nearly every elected office in the country, from the presidency on down to many local offices.

The effects of the direct primary are so *widespread*—and so *toxic*—that those effects are slowly killing the political life of our country.

* * *

The direct primary gives rise to an entire galaxy of myths and assumptions about our political process.

The most dangerous effect of the direct primary is that it deceives the people into looking to political leaders for salvation.

It persuades us to turn away from the institutions that made our country great, and to seek greatness in our leaders.

It deceives us into yearning for a political messiah.

The direct primary's wide-ranging effects on our perception of government—and of our role in it—make it far more than a mere provision of election law.

It doesn't occur to most people, for example, that liberty and rule of law are *perfectly at odds* with the servile attitude toward candidates and elected officials that prevails today, an attitude fostered entirely by the direct primary system.

We've never been more smitten by charismatic leaders who promise to rise above the fray, as we are today.

And yet we've never been more consistently double-crossed by political charlatans.

We've never been more enamored with political leaders who masquerade as tribunes of the people.

And yet we've never been more betrayed by official deception, white lies, and empty promises.

At the root of all this subtlety, cunning, and deception is the direct primary system itself: a master of deception not unlike the leaders it foists on the people.

* * *

Today, as Americans go about their daily lives, a state of normalcy *seems* to prevail.

In the public life of our country, our affairs seem to move along in fits and starts, just as they always have.

If you look at the reelection rate of incumbents throughout the United States, this impression of *extreme normalcy* is only further reinforced.

Roman historian Eric Gruen paints a similar picture of people going about daily life as usual in his study *The Last Generation of the Roman Republic.*

According to Gruen's analysis, there was nothing especially out of the ordinary in the political condition of Rome during the last decades of the Republic.

Gruen takes it as a sign of popular satisfaction that "the Republic's final two decades show that more than 80 percent of the consuls had forebears in that office."[1]

It is a chilling irony that some future historian might look back on the condition of the United States today—especially at the entrenched incumbency and political dynasticism—and take it as a sign that there was nothing especially out of the ordinary happening.

Today in America, even as our political institutions seem outwardly to function as they always have—even as we continue to reelect the same people *over and over*—public confidence in our political system is reaching a point of crisis *by virtually any measure.*

In the case of Rome, how can we account for the rapid descent from a scene of tranquility to the political chaos that broke out, in the Republic's final decades?

The key to unraveling this paradox lies in clearly distinguishing between three very different conditions: popular satisfaction, the stability of political institutions, and the persistent reelection of incumbents.

While Gruen assumed these conditions to be one and the same, these conditions are quite distinct.

When Gruen speaks of the "persistent success"[2] of the Roman elite, he's not observing popular satisfaction *or* political stability. He's merely observing the outward effect of incumbents' skill at winning reelection.

Since the "persistent success" of the Roman elite lies at the center of Gruen's scene of tranquility, it's worth examining the probable cause of that success.

Gruen casts doubt on the notion that "familial ties, connections, wealth, and aristocratic heritage"[3] had much to with the high reelection rate of incumbents.

Gruen points instead to "the claims of the populace, the need to promote popular interests, and the influence the *populus Romanus* could exercise upon electoral results."[4]

If we peel back the layers of Roman constitutional history, the reason for the "persistent success" of the Roman political class was no different than the reason for the success of political class in modern America.

In *The American Commonwealth*, James Bryce describes "the plan of the Romans," of which he says: "the *comitia* (primary assemblies) were convoked only to elect magistrates and pass laws, [the laws being] short, clear, and submitted...without possibility of amendment."[5]

The *comitia* were thus a kind of direct primary combined with a referendum.

We know from historical accounts of the late Republic that tumult, violence, and mob rule plagued the *comitia*.

We also know that confusion and disorder in the *comitia* allowed demagogues to rise to power.

The effects of a direct primary, combined with the tumult of a primary assembly, seem to have conspired to unravel the Roman political institutions.

Political leaders emerged who pursued power for its own sake, and not for any cause greater than their own ambition. They did whatever seemed necessary to win office; and they exercised power without scruple.

In the final years of the Republic, as the system broke down, Roman politics became a brutal war of all against all: the "mischiefs of faction" unleashed on an epic scale.

Given the chaos that ensued, who was the man who could have saved the Republic? Cicero with his speeches? Caesar with his army? Brutus with his dagger?[6]

The story of the decline and fall of the Roman Republic is indeed a story of flawed men, but to a larger degree it is a cautionary story of failed institutions.

In truth, no one could have saved the Republic by his own will, because no one could tame the chaos brought about by the failure of Roman political institutions.

If indeed the fall of the Republic was born of the repudiation of sound institutions, then only by fixing the problem at that level could the demise of the Republic have been averted.

* * *

The framers of our Constitution knew the history of the Roman Republic well, and they did what they could to place our system on firmer ground.

Through the machinery of the Constitution, they sought to establish a system that would "last for ages."[7]

They wanted to create a system that would arrest mankind's periodic flirtation with tyranny for all time.

Today, there are many people who claim to know better than the framers of our Constitution, but they deceive themselves and ruin our country.

Amidst signs and wonders that our institutions are coming apart at the seams, we could do far worse than look back at what the framers did, and *why* they did it.

Are we living through the last generation of the American republic?

The answer to that question is not given because it depends entirely on what we do.

While the crisis we face today may *seem* overwhelming, the real problem we need to fix is actually very *specific*.

The indirect primary would *eliminate* most problems that afflict our system of self-government today.

Like the ancient Israelites who sometimes turned away from their covenant with God, we have strayed from the principles of our Constitution.[8]

Yet the principles remain constant, waiting to restore our country, if only we would turn toward them again.

Notes

Introduction – Is America Governable?
The introduction title comes from the title of a conference held at the University of Texas Law School on January 24-26, 2013. The conference, organized by Sanford Levinson, included eminent scholars, journalists, and political figures from around the country. Those discussions helped to distill the core thesis of this book.

1. Pietro S. Nivola and David W. Brady, eds., *Red and Blue Nation?: Characteristics and Causes of America's Polarized Politics* (2006), 1.
2. Ronald Brownstein, *The Second Civil War: How Extreme Partisanship has Paralyzed Washington and Polarized America* (2007), 1.
3. Thomas E. Mann and Norman J. Ornstein, *It's Even Worse Than It Looks: How the American Constitutional System Collided with the New Politics of Extremism* (2012; 2013), xxi.
4. Fareed Zakaria, *The Future of Freedom: Illiberal Democracy at Home and Abroad* (2003), 184.
5. James Carville and Stanley B. Greenberg, *It's the Middle Class, Stupid!* (2012), cover.
6. Lawrence Lessig, *Republic, Lost: How Money Corrupts Congress—and a Plan to Stop It* (2011), 7.
7. Lawrence Lessig, TED talk (April 2013), http://www.ted.com/talks/lawrence_lessig_we_the_people_ and_the_republic_we_must_reclaim.html.
8. Kenneth Lieberthal and Wang Jisi, "Addressing U.S.-China Strategic Distrust" (Brookings Institute, March 2012).
9. Regarding the severity of declining public confidence in American political institutions, see Sanford Levinson, *Framed: America's 51 Constitutions and the Crisis of Governance* (2012), 2-3.
10. See Gallop, "Congressional Approval Sinks to Record Low: Current Approval at 9%," November 12, 2013; and Rasmussen, "Just 8% of Voters Think Congress is Doing a Good or Excellent Job," January 8, 2014.

Part I
1. John Locke, *Second Treatise of Government* (1689), chap. 18.

Chapter 1 – Uncontrolled Search and Seizure
1. M. H. Smith, *The Writs of Assistance Case* (1978), 552.

2. Ibid., 553.
3. John Adams quoted in Leonard W. Levy, *Origins of the Bill of Rights* (1999), 158.
4. Massachusetts Constitution of 1780; Philip B. Kurland and Ralph Lerner, eds., *The Founder's Constitution* (1987), 5: 237.
5. North Carolina Declaration of Rights of 1776; Virginia Declaration of Rights of 1776; Neil H. Cogan, *The Complete Bill of Rights* (1997), 234-35.
6. James Risen and Eric Lichtblau, "Bush Lets U.S. Spy on Callers Without Courts," *New York Times,* December 16, 2005.
7. Glenn Greenwald, "NSA Collecting Phone Records of Millions of Verizon Customers Daily," *The Guardian* , June 6, 2013.

Chapter 2 – Taxation without Representation
1. See Gordon S. Wood, *The Creation of the American Republic, 1776-1787* (1969; 1998), 166.
2. Quoted in Edmund S. Morgan, *The Stamp Act Crisis: Prologue to Revolution* (1953; 1962), 93.
3. Quoted in ibid., 105.
4. Quoted in ibid., 106.
5. Quoted in ibid., 142.
6. Quoted in ibid., 143.
7. Lawrence Henry Gipson, *The Coming of the Revolution, 1763-1775* (1954), 104.
8. Ezra Klein, "No, Congress Isn't Trying to Exempt Itself from Obamacare," *Washington Post,* April 25, 2013.

Chapter 3 – Disarmament of Free Citizens
1. Stephen P. Halbrooke, *The Founder's Second Amendment: Origins of the Right to Bear Arms* (2012), chap. 1.
2. Quoted in ibid., 11.
3. The English Bill of Rights (1689); Carl Stephenson and Frederick George Marcham, *Sources of English Constitutional History: A Selection of Documents from A.D. 600 to the Present* (1937), 600-601.
4. Abigail Adams quoted in Halbrooke, ibid., 97.
5. Pennsylvania Constitution of 1776, Declaration of Rights, Art. 13; Kurland and Lerner, *Founder's Constitution,* 5:210.
6. Ibid.
7. Virginia Declaration of Rights of 1776; Neil H. Cogan, *The Complete Bill of Rights* (1997), 185.
8. See Sanford Levinson, "The Embarrassing Second Amendment," in Les Adams, *The Second Amendment Primer* (2013), 201-3 (originally published in *Yale Law Journal* [vol. 99, 1989]).
9. Ibid.
10. Halbrooke, ibid., 5, 330, 334; and Levinson, ibid., 200.
11. Halbrooke, ibid., 5, 323-26; and Levinson, ibid., 198.

12. See Halbrooke, ibid., 329.
13. See Stephen P. Halbrook, *That Every Man Be Armed* (1984; 2013), chap. 1; and Levinson, ibid., 201-2.
14. Plato, *The Republic*, translated by Benjamin Jowett (1941), bk. 1.
15. Ibid., bk. 5.
16. Aristotle, *The Politics*, translated by T. A. Sinclair, revised by Trevor J. Saunders (1962; 1992), 124 (emphasis added).
17. Niccolo Machiavelli, *The Prince*, translated by W. K. Marriott (1958), chap. 12.
18. Alexis de Tocqueville, *Democracy in America*, translated by Henry Reeve (1945), introduction.
19. See Stephen P. Halbrook, *Gun Control in the Third Reich: Disarming the Jews and 'Enemies of the State'* (2013).

Part II
1. Alexander Hamilton in Alexander Hamilton, John Jay, and James Madison, *The Federalist*, George W. Carey and James McClellan, eds., (2001), 443,447.
2. James Madison in ibid., 126, 256.

Chapter 4 – The Secret Thread of American Political History
1. U.S. Const. amd. XII.
2. Charles Pinckney in Max Farrand, *The Records of the Federal Convention*, 4 vols. (1937; 1987), 1:358.
3. Roger Sherman in Farrand, *Records*, 2:29.
4. U.S. Const. art. II, sec. 1, cl. 3; and U.S. Const. amd. XII.
5. Ironically, the congressional caucus system of nomination stimulated demand for the Twelfth Amendment, as seen in the election of 1800.
6. Frederick W. Whitridge, *Caucus System* (1883), 9.
7. The Democratic-Republican Party's control of Congress was also due to causes in the electoral system, such as the use of statewide general ticket elections to elect the House delegations of many states. This era of "nonpartisan" one-party rule at the national level is commemorated by historians as the "Era of Good Feelings." But "nonpartisanship" only left the door open for sectional tensions to rise.
8. Charles S. Thompson, *An Essay on the Rise and Fall of the Congressional Caucus* (1902), 37.
9. The framers of the Constitution had concerns about the legislative selection of the executive which the congressional caucus system only served to demonstrate. See James Wilson, Gouverneur Morris, and Elbridge Gerry in Farrand, *Records*, 2:30, 2:29 and 1: 175.
10. Fredrick Dallinger, *Nominations for Elective Office in the United States* (1897), 21-25.
11. Dallinger, *Nominations for Elective Office*, 28.

12. Congressional Quarterly, Inc., *Congressional Quarterly's Guide to U.S. Elections* (3rd ed., 1994), 12, 294.
13. Richard J. Ellis, *The Development of the American Presidency* (2013), 35.
14. Ibid., 35.
15. This is still how the process works today in many states. The major difference is that convention delegates do not have the authority to nominate candidates for elected office.
16. In urban areas, the county party conventions were (and still are today) often subdivided by legislative district (for example, into state senate district conventions).
17. Ibid., 130.
18. Ibid., 31, 481.
19. *Acts and Resolutions Adopted by the Legislature of Florida* (1901), chap. 5014.
20. *Laws of Wisconsin* (1905), chap. 369; Walter Earl Spahr, *The Wisconsin Primary Election Law* (1917), 103-05.
21. *Laws of Pennsylvania, Extraordinary Session of 1906* (1906), 36-44.
22. *State of Oregon Session Laws* (1911), 19-23; Allen H. Eaton, *The Oregon System: The Story of Direct Legislation in Oregon* (1912), 108.
23. Louise Overacker, *The Presidential Primary* (1926), 10-13.
24. Overacker, *The Presidential Primary* (1926), 13; Charles Merriam and Louise Overacker, *Primary Elections* (1928), app. A; CQ, Guide to Elections, 481.
25. Overacker, *Presidential Primary*, 214-19; see also CQ, *Guide to Elections*, 493-95.
26. See *Merriam-Webster's 11th Collegiate Dictionary*, s.v. "smoke-filled room."

Chapter 5 – Rotation in Office and Entrenched Incumbency

1. Eric Matthew Glassman, Erin Hemlin, and Amber Hope Wilhelm, "Congressional Careers: Service Tenure and Patterns of Member Service, 1789-2011." Congressional Research Service, January 7, 2011.
2. Ibid., 4.
3. The data on presidential and vice presidential succession is drawn from CQ's *Guide to Elections* (3rd ed., 1994).
4. Platform quoted in CQ, *Guide to Elections*, 72.
5. Theodore Roosevelt, *The Rough Riders; an Autobiography* (Library of America ed., 2004), 644.
6. William Safire, *Safire's Political Dictionary* (1968; 2008), s.v. "hat in the ring." The phrase was coined by Roosevelt himself in 1912.
7. We could get into technicalities about whether Roosevelt's succession to the presidency after McKinley's assassination

constituted a full first term. But under the terms later adopted via the Twenty-Second Amendment, Roosevelt's first term would have counted; thus Roosevelt would've been prohibited from running in 1912.

8. Although Vice President John Calhoun was on the ballot for reelection in 1828, this exception did not violate the rule. Calhoun was on the ballot practically by default: the congressional caucus had ceased after 1824, and no national convention was assembled in 1828. *Thus no vice presidential nomination was made that year.* Nor is this exception a mere quibbling over technicalities: rather, it suggests that the national convention system (first used in the 1832 election) was the best for securing rotation in office of all the nominating systems we've ever had. The one-term tradition in the vice presidency was abandoned at the same time the presidential direct primary took root.

9. See chap. 9 below.

10. On this critical point, see David Butler and Bruce Cain, *Congressional Redistricting* (1992), 13: "we should distinguish the claim that *redistricting is the cause of the incumbency advantage* from the claim that *incumbents seek and often obtain advantages from redistricting*" (emphasis in original).

11. Froma Harrop. "Americans Don't Need Political Mini Royals." *Creators Syndicate* , August 6, 2013.

12. Political dynasticism existed prior to 1910 (and thus prior to the direct primary) only under the congressional caucus system of nomination. John Quincy Adams was the first son to succeed his father to the presidency, a feat not repeated until George W. Bush followed George H. W. Bush to the presidency under the direct primary system.

13. T. R. Fehrenbach, *Lone Star: A History of Texas and the Texans* (2000), 646.

14. Dan T. Carter, *The Politics of Rage* (1995; 2000), chap. 9.

15. Rick Farmer, ed., *Legislating Without Experience: Case Studies in State Legislative Term Limits* (2007), 79, 97, 154, 167.

16. See James Davis, *National Conventions in an Age of Party Reform* (1983), xii-xiv, 6, 10.

Chapter 6 – Distribution and Concentration of Power

1. Today, Congress more often aids and abets the expansion of executive power by delegating administrative rulemaking powers and by acquiescing to "legislation by fiat" in the form of executive orders and signing statements. All of these unconstitutional methods of lawmaking are unprecedented in scope and frequency today.

2. James Madison in Hamilton, Jay, and Madison, *Federalist*, 268.

3. James Madison in ibid., 235 (emphasis added).

4. Tocqueville, *Democracy in America*, bk.2, sec. 4, chap. 5.

5. Christopher H. Hoebeke, *The Road to Mass Democracy: Original Intent and the Seventeenth Amendment* (1995; 2013), 13, 16, 19, 111.
6. See Ernst C. Meyer, *Nominating Systems: Direct Primaries Versus Conventions in the United States* (1902), chaps. 3 and 5.
7. William Samuel Johnson in Farrand, *Records*, 1:461.
8. U.S. Const. amd. X.
9. See Ralph A. Rossum, *Federalism, the Supreme Court, and the Seventeenth Amendment* (2001), 248-50.
10. Neil MacNeil and Richard A. Baker, *The American Senate: An Insider's History* (2013), 23-27, 35; George B. Galloway, *Congress at the Crossroads* (1946), 38-39; Congressional Quarterly, Inc., *Guide to Congress* (6th ed. 2008), 117-19.
11. James Caesar, *Presidential Selection: Theory and Development* (1979), 7.
12. Michael Nelson, ed., *Guide to the Presidency* (4th ed. 2008), 902-03, 1064-70.
13. The Kennedy administration's hiring process features prominently in David Halberstam's *The Best and the Brightest* (1972).
14. See Arthur M. Schlesinger, *The Imperial Presidency* (1973; 3rd ed. 2004).
15. Terry Sanford, *A Danger of Democracy: The Presidential Nominating Process* (1981), 1-6.
16. See Theodore H. White, *The Making of the President, 1960* (1961).
17. This was true of both major parties, for the first time. See CQ, *Guide to Elections*, 481.

Chapter 7 – Self-Government and the Permanent Campaign
1. Sidney Blumenthal, *The Permanent Campaign: Inside the World of Elite Political Operatives* (1980), 7.
2. Norman J. Ornstein and Thomas E. Mann, *The Permanent Campaign and Its Future* (2000), vii.
3. Gene Healy, *The Cult of the Presidency: America's Dangerous Devotion to Executive Power* (2008; 2009), 301.
4. Jeffrey Tullis, *The Rhetorical Presidency* (1987), 4.
5. Ibid., 144.
6. Tocqueville, *Democracy in America*, bk. 1, chap. 8.

Part III
Chapter 8 – The Beginning of a Congressional Revolution
1. See Stephen Ansolabehere, Shigeo Hirano, and James M. Snyder, Jr., "What Did the Direct Primary Do to Party Loyalty in Congress?" Working paper (March 2004).
2. U.S. Const. art. I, sec. 5, cl. 3.
3. Charles Atkinson, *The Committee on Rules and the Overthrow of Cannon* (1911), 8-9. Also noteworthy is that *Robert's Rules* says

of committee appointments that "appointment by the chair [is] the method that should usually be adopted in very large assemblies." See Henry M. Robert, *Robert's Rules of Order* (1921), 128.
4. George R. Brown, *The Leadership of Congress* (1922), 2, 196.
5. See U.S. Department of the Treasury, *Annual Report of the Secretary of the Treasury on the State of the Finances, for the Fiscal Year Ended June 30, 1956*, Treasury Department Document No. 3203 (1957), Table 2.

Chapter 9 – The Rebirth of the Rotten Boroughs
1. See David Butler and Bruce Cain, *Congressional Redistricting* (1992), 4.
2. See, for example, *Davis v. Bandemer*, 478 U.S. 109 (1986); and *Vieth v. Jubelirer*, 541 U.S. 267 (2004).
3. Norman J. Ornstein, Thomas E. Mann, and Michael J. Malbin, *Vital Statistics on Congress 2008* (2008), 63.
4. Elmer Griffith, *The Rise and Development of the Gerrymander* (1907), 73.
5. Ibid., 3.
6. Ibid., 120.
7. Farrand, *Records*, 1:450, 491.
8. Ibid., I, 450, 457.
9. This violated the principle of contiguity, which requires that all points within a district should be reachable without leaving the district.
10. This violated the principle of compactness, which requires that every point along the boundary should be as close as possible to the center of the district.
11. Apportionment Act of 1842, 5 Stat. 491 (1842).
12. Apportionment Act of 1872, 17 Stat. 192 (1872).
13. Apportionment Act of 1901, 31 Stat. 733 (1901).
14. Apportionment Act of 1911, 37 Stat. 13 (1911).
15. Apportionment Act of 1929, 46 Stat. 21 (1929).
16. See Charles W. Eagles, *Democracy Delayed: Congressional Reapportionment and Urban-Rural Conflict in the 1920s* (1990).
17. *Wood v. Broom*, 287 U.S. 1 (1932).
18. *Colegrove v. Green*, 328 U.S. 549, 556 (1946).
19. See Butler and Cain, ibid., 26-27
20. Gene Graham, *One Man, One Vote: Baker v. Carr and the American Levellers* (1972), 14-18.
21. Ibid., 56.
22. Ibid., 29, 139.
23. Ibid., 96.
24. *Baker v. Carr*, 369 U.S. 186 (1962).
25. Graham, *One Man, One Vote*, 170, 261.
26. See Raoul Berger, *Government by Judiciary: The Transformation of the Fourteenth Amendment* (2nd ed. 1997), chap. 5.

27. *Gray v. Sanders*, 372 U.S. 368, 381 (1963).
28. *Wesberry v. Sanders*, 376 U.S. 1 (1964); *Reynolds v. Sims*, 377 U.S. 533 (1964); *Avery v. Midland County, Texas*, 390 U.S. 474 (1968).
29. The Court's attack on the "little federal plans," by which state senates were apportioned by county, is one example of this. The "little federal plans" were modeled after the U.S. Senate's apportionment by state.
30. *Lucas v. Forty-Fourth General Assembly of Colorado*, 377 U.S. 713 (1964).
31. *Kirkpatrick v. Preisler*, 394 U.S. 526 (1969).
32. *Karcher v. Daggett*, 426 U.S. 725 (1983).
33. *Badham v. March Fong Eu*, 694 F.Supp 664, 670 (1988); *Badham v. Eu*, 488 U.S. 1024 (1989).
34. *Kirkpatrick v. Preisler*, 394 U.S. 526, 530 (1969).
35. *Gaffney v. Cummings*, 412 U.S. 735 (1973).
36. *Davis v. Bandemer*, 478 U.S. 109 (1986); *Vieth v. Jubelirer*, 541 U.S. 267 (2004). See also Butler and Cain, ibid., 39.
37. Regarding the problem of the criteria courts might use to ensure neutral redistricting, see Butler and Cain, ibid., 148-52.

Chapter 10 – The Development of a "Matrix of Dictatorship"

1. William Maclay, *The Journal of William Maclay, United States Senator from Pennsylvania, 1789-1791* (1965), 114.
2. See *Blake v. United States*, 103 U.S. 227 (1881); *Wallace v. United States*, 257 U.S. 541 (1922); and *Myers v. United States*, 272 U.S. 52 (1926).
3. The acquittal was made by only one vote; it nonetheless upheld the long chain of precedents stretching back to the Decision of 1789.
4. James D. Richardson, *A Compilation of the Messages and Papers of the Presidents, 1789-1897* (1897), 3:1012.
5. The phrase is attributed to Senator William Marcy of New York. See Richard Hofstader, *The Idea of Party System* (1969), 250n37; and Elihu Root, *Addresses on Government and Citizenship* (1916), 51.
6. Carl Russell Fish, *The Civil Service and the Patronage* (1905), 172.
7. Edward Cary, *The Civil Service: The Merit System—the Spoils System* (1903), 6.
8. Civil Service Act of 1883 ("Pendleton Act"), 22 Stat. 403.
9. Paul van Riper, *History of the United States Civil Service* (1958), 101-3. William Dudley Foulke, *Fighting the Spoilsmen: Reminiscences of the Civil Service Reform Movement* (1919), 9-10, 327-29; Fish, *The Civil Service and the Patronage*, 220-21.
10. Executive Order dated July 27, 1897.
11. Executive Order dated May 29, 1902.

12. Lloyd-LaFollette Act of 1912, 37 Stat. 3552 (1912); Van Riper, *History of the United States Civil Service*, 216-17.
13. Edward S. Corwin, *The President: Office and Powers* (1948), 353.

Chapter 11 – The Growth of "Legislative Blackmail"
1. U.S. Const. art. I, sec. 5, cl. 3.
2. U.S. Const. art. I, sec. 5, cl. 2.
3. Farrand, *Records*, 1:421.
4. Richard A. Arenberg and Robert B. Dove, *Defending the Filibuster: The Soul of the Senate* (2012), 5; Sarah A. Binder and Steven S. Smith, *Politics or Principle: Filibustering in the United States Senate* (1997), 34-37; Henry M. Robert, *Robert's Rules of Order, Newly Revised* (11th ed. 2011), xli.
5. Binder and Smith, *Politics or Principle*, 38.
6. Franklin L. Burdette, *Filibustering in the Senate* (1940; 1965), 22-3.
7. Quoted in ibid., 69.
8. Ibid.,72.
9. Ibid.
10. Francis Butler Simkins, *Pitchfork Ben Tillman, South Carolinian* (1944; 2002), 229.
11. Burdette, *Filibustering in the Senate*, 83-4.
12. George B. Galloway, *Congress at the Crossroads* (1946), 38-39.
13. Statement issued by Woodrow Wilson quoted in Thomas W. Ryley, *A Little Group of Willful Men: A Study of Congressional-Presidential Authority* (1975), 3.
14. Congressional Quarterly, Inc., *Guide to Congress* (6th ed. 2008), 246, Table 5-2.
15. William Fulbright quoted in ibid., 247.

Chapter 12 – The Transformation of the "Money Power"
1. See Richard H. Timberlake, *Monetary Policy in the United States: An Intellectual and Institutional History* (1993), xix.
2. There are actually more than two points of correlation between the institutional transformations in our monetary and nominating systems. There are at least five (with a sixth unfolding right now), but covering all of them is beyond the scope of this chapter.
3. James D. Richardson, *A Compilation of the Messages and Papers of the Presidents, 1789-1897* (1897), 3:1139.
4. Thomas Hart Benton, *Thirty Years' View* (1874; 2 vols.), 1:187.
5. The frontrunner for the 1844 Democratic nomination, Martin Van Buren, was rejected due to his unyielding opposition to the annexation of Texas. Lewis Cass of Michigan, next in line, was in favor of annexing Texas, but many Democrats thought his soundness on the bank question was in doubt. James K. Polk was not considered until the eighth ballot. He won the nomination by the ninth ballot because his views on these key issues were

acceptable to both factions. Polk's unexpected nomination made him the first "dark horse" candidate. But the fact that his nomination was a compromise did not mean that he was an obscure or mediocre man. Walter K. Borneman, *Polk: The Man Who Transformed the Presidency and America* (2008; 2009), 99-103; Congressional Quarterly, Inc., *Guide to U.S. Elections* (3rd ed., 1994), 29, 40; Willard Carl Klunder, *Lewis Cass and the Politics of Moderation* (1996), 124; Nicholas Biddle, *The Correspondence of Nicholas Biddle Dealing With National Affairs, 1807-1844*, ed. Reginald C. McGrane (1919), 160n2.

6. Borneman, *Polk*, 226-27; Paul H. Bergeron, *The Presidency of James K. Polk* (1987), 192-93.

7. Timberlake, *Monetary Policy in the United States*, 252.

8. Socialist Party platforms of 1904 and 1912 quoted in CQ, *Guide to U.S. Elections*, 74, 78.

9. Margaret G. Myers, *A Financial History of the United States*, 245-49.

10. See A. Barton Hepburn, *A History of the Currency of the United States* (1903; 1924), chap. 21.

11. See U.S. Department of the Treasury, *Annual Report of the Secretary of the Treasury on the State of the Finances, for the Fiscal Year Ended June 30, 1956*, Treasury Department Document No. 3203 (1957), Table 2, Table 16.

12. Elihu Root, *Addresses on Government and Citizenship* (1916), 336.

13. Ibid., 268-69.

14. Ibid., 252.

15. Woodrow Wilson, *Constitutional Government in the United States* (1908), 221.

16. Ludwig von Mises, *The Theory of Money and Credit* (1912; 2009), 414.

Chapter 13 – The Rise of "Government by Judiciary"

1. *Black's Law Dictionary* (7th ed. 1999), s.v. "Certiorari, Writ of" (emphasis added).

2. Judiciary Act of 1789, 1 Stat. 73 (1789).

3. John Jay quoted in Kermit L. Hall, James W. Ely and Joel B. Grossman, *Oxford Companion to the Supreme Court* (2nd ed. 2005), s.v. "Jay, John."

4. Removal Act of 1833, 4 Stat. 633 (1833).

5. See Removal Act of 1863, 12 Stat. 754 (1863); 14 Stat. 306 (1866); 14 Stat. 558 (1867); 15 Stat. 227 (1868); and 17 Stat. 44 (1872).

6. Removal Act of 1875, 18 Stat. 470 (1875).

7. Felix Frankfurter and James M. Landis, *The Business of the Supreme Court: A Study in the Federal Judicial System* (1927; 2007), 60.

8. Ibid.

9. This section relies heavily on the account given by Edward A. Hartnett in "Questioning Certiorari: Some Reflections Seventy-Five Years After the Judges' Bill." *Columbia Law Review* 100: 1643-1738.

10. Quoted in ibid., 1661.

11. Quoted in ibid., 1661.

12. Quoted in ibid., 1704.

13. *Gitlow v. New York*, 268 U.S. 652 (1925).

14. See "Amendments Passed in the House of Representatives August 24, 1789" in Levy W. Levy, *Origins of the Bill of Rights* (1999), 289 (emphasis added).

15. See Louis Brandies' dissent in *New State Ice Co. v Liebmann*, 285 U.S. 262, 311 (1932).

16. Alexander Hamilton in Hamilton, Jay, and Madison, *Federalist*, 402.

17. See Raoul Berger, *Government by Judiciary: The Transformation of the Fourteenth Amendment* (1977; 1997).

18. Along these lines, see Charles Gardner Geyh, *When Courts & Congress Collide* (2006; 2008), 67; Edward Keynes and Randall K. Miller, *The Court vs. Congress: Prayer, Busing, and Abortion* (1989); and (ironically) Raoul Berger, *Congress v. the Supreme Court* (1969).

Chapter 14 – The Prevalence of "Ideological Polarization"

1. Richard Hofstadter. *The Idea of a Party System: The Rise of Legitimate Opposition in the United States, 1780-1840* (1969), 12.

2. John Adams, *The Works of John Adams*, edited by Charles Francis Adams (1854), IX, 511 (emphasis added).

3. James Madison in Farrand, *Records*, 1:135 (emphasis added).

4. Martin van Buren, *The Autobiography of Martin Van Buren*, edited by John C. Fitzpatrick (1920), 125.

5. Ibid.

6. See E. E. Schattschneider, *Party Government* (1942), chap. 5; V. O. Key, *Politics, Parties, and Pressure Groups* (1942; 4th ed. 1958), chap. 8; Maurice Duverger, *Political Parties: Their Organization and Activity in the Modern State*, trans. by Barbara and Robert North (1951; 1963), 203-20.

7. This is based on empirical observation of the data available in Kenneth C. Martis, *The Historical Atlas of Political Parties in the United States Congress, 1789-1989* (1989).

8. As mentioned above, this is the system that yielded one-party rule at the national level.

9. See "Goodbye to the Permanent Majority?" *The Economist* (Nov. 4, 2006), 27.

10. See Lisa Jane Disch, *The Tyranny of the Two-Party System* (2002).

11. See Eldon Cobb Evans, *A History of the Australian Ballot System in the United States* (1917); and Lionel E. Fredman, *The Australian Ballot: The Story of an American Reform* (1968).

12. See Leon D. Epstein, *Political Parties in the American Mold* (1986), 156-7.

13. Congressional Quarterly, Inc., *Guide to U.S. Elections* (3rd ed. 1994), 385, 443, 267.

14. Martis, *Historical Atlas of Political Parties*, 149-57.

15. Ibid.

16. Simon L. Adler, *The Direct Primary in New York State* (1909), 2.

17. Thomas E. Mann and Norman J. Ornstein, *It's Even Worse Than It Looks: How the American Constitutional System Collided with the New Politics of Extremism* (2012; 2013), 151 (emphasis added).

18. Robert Richie, Steven Hill, et. al., *Reflecting All of Us: The Case for Proportional Representation* (1999), 13 (emphasis added).

19. See Ferdinand Hermens, *Democracy or Anarchy?: A Study of Proportional Representation* (1941; 1972), chaps. 7-11.

20. Hermens, *Democracy or Anarchy*, chap. 6, 7, 14-16; for an alternative view (less substantiated by the facts), see Samuel Issacharoff, Pamela S. Karlan, and Richard H. Pildes, *The Law of Democracy: Legal Structure of the Political Process* (1998; 2nd ed. 2002), chap. 13.

21. Hermens, *Democracy or Anarchy*, 403-14.

22. Charles Merriam and Louise Overacker, *Primary Elections* (1928), 274. This book was published nearly two decades after Merriam's original study, *Primary Elections* (1908).

23. Merriam and Overacker, *Primary Elections*, 212, 227-30.

Part IV
Chapter 15 – The Citizen's Role in Self-Government

1. County conventions are sometimes subdivided into smaller conventions—for example, into senate district conventions—in highly populous urban counties of the United States.

2. See *O'Brien v. Brown*, 409 U.S. 1 (1972); *Cousins v. Wigoda*, 419 U.S. 477 (1975); *Democratic Party of the United States v. LaFollette*, 450 U.S. 107 (1981); *Tashjian v. Republican Party of Connecticut*, 479 U.S. 208 (1986). Each of these cases affirms the power of political parties to determine their primary election and delegate selection rules.

3. Incidentally, Iowa is considered a caucus state, but its informal party straw polls are reported by the media as if they were the results of a direct primary, and the effect of the party straw poll in binding delegates ends up being very similar.

4. In reality, this is simplifying the process somewhat. Few national convention delegates would be directly elected. Most would be chosen by intermediary state or congressional district conventions. In any case, direct election of a national convention delegate from

an area the size of a congressional district would cause the delegate to incur enormous expenses. The point of this account is to illustrate the underlying principle: delegates' names should replace candidates' names on the primary ballot. In the case of the presidency, this might be done by simply eliminating the candidate preference vote and placing congressional district convention delegates' names on the ballot. The congressional district convention would then select the number of national convention delegates and alternate delegates apportioned to that congressional district.

Conclusion – Are We Rome?

1. Erich S. Gruen, *The Last Generation of the Roman Republic* (1974; 1995), ix.
2. Ibid., x.
3. This is quoted as a counterclaim in ibid., x.
4. Ibid., x.
5. James Bryce, *The American Commonwealth* (1888; 1995), 1:140.
6. For perspective, see Plutarch. "Life of Cicero," "Life of Caesar," and "Life of Brutus" in *The Lives of Noble Grecians and Romans* (1932).
7. James Madison in Farrand, *Records*, 1:422.
8. As to the "covenant theology" implicit in the Constitution, see Sanford Levinson, *Constitutional Faith* (2011), 5, 11-12; and Russell Kirk, *The Roots of American Order* (1978), 25-30.

About the Author

Carl Jarvis is among today's leading authorities on the history of American political institutions.

His writings, talks, and media appearances are transforming how people think about the American political process—and, how they engage in the process.

His unique approach to American political history shows ordinary citizens how they can have a real impact, without running for office or joining a protest.

He is a former naval officer, an alumnus of the Naval Nuclear Propulsion Program, and a graduate of Rensselaer Polytechnic Institute.

His interest in American constitutional history began nearly two decades ago when he took the oath of office to "support and defend the Constitution."

Carl is a longtime resident of Houston, Texas, where he lives with his wife and three children.

Visit Carl at **www.CarlJarvis.org**.

Looking for More?

- Take the "U.S. of D." survey:

    www.USofD.com/survey

- Get the audio version:

    www.USofD.com/audio

- Signup for free bonus materials, updates, and e-newsletter:

    www.USofD.com/bonus

- Get volume discount pricing for bulk purchases of *The United States of Dysfunction*:

    www.USofD.com/discount

Made in the USA
Lexington, KY
09 July 2014